Ethical Problems
In Higher Education

Occupational
Ethics Series

Norman Bowie Business Ethics
Peter A. French Ethics in Government
Tom L. Beauchamp & Laurence B. McCullough Medical Ethics
Mary Ann Carroll, Henry G. Schneider & George R. Wesley
Ethics in the Practice of Psychology
Deborah G. Johnson Computer Ethics
George M. Robinson & Janice Moulton Ethical Problems In Higher Education

Elizabeth Beardsley and John Atwell,
Series Editors

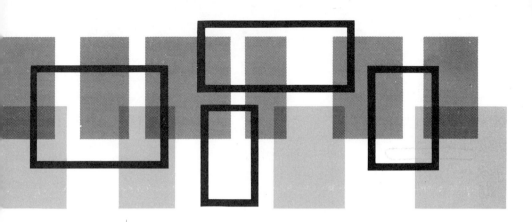

Ethical Problems in Higher Education

GEORGE M. ROBINSON
JANICE MOULTON

PRENTICE-HALL, INC., Englewood Cliffs, New Jersey 07632

Library of Congress Cataloging in Publication Data

Robinson, George M.
  Ethical problems in higher education.

  Bibliography: p. 99
  Includes index.
  1. Education, Higher—United States—Moral and
ethical aspects. 2. College teachers, Professional
ethics for—United States. 3. Community and college—
United States—Moral and ethical aspects. 4. Research—
United States—Moral and ethical aspects. I. Moulton,
Janice   II. Title.
LA227.3.R64 1985   174'.937   84-17932
ISBN 0-13-290198-6

Editorial/production supervision and
  interior design: Kate Kelly
Manufacturing buyer: Harry P. Baisley

Printed in the United States of America

10 9 8 7 6 5 4 3 2 1

ISBN 0-13-290198-6   01

PRENTICE-HALL INTERNATIONAL, INC., *London*
PRENTICE-HALL OF AUSTRALIA PTY. LIMITED, *Sydney*
EDITORA PRENTICE-HALL DO BRASIL, LTDA., *Rio de Janeiro*
PRENTICE-HALL CANADA INC., *Toronto*
PRENTICE-HALL HISPANOAMERICANA, S. A., *Mexico*
PRENTICE-HALL OF INDIA PRIVATE LIMITED, *New Delhi*
PRENTICE-HALL OF JAPAN, INC., *Tokyo*
PRENTICE-HALL OF SOUTHEAST ASIA PTE. LTD., *Singapore*
WHITEHALL BOOKS LIMITED, *Wellington, New Zealand*

Contents

Prentice-Hall Series in Occupational Ethics

An increasing number of philosophers are coming to appreciate the value of making our discipline constructively available to those whose lives are chiefly focused on some form of practical activity. It is natural that philosophers specializing in ethics should be in the forefront of this movement toward "applied philosophy." In both writing and teaching many leading ethical theorists are currently dealing with concrete issues in individual and social life.

While this change has been taking place within the philosophic community, practitioners in various fields have (for several complex reasons) turned their attention to the ethical dimensions of their own activities. Whether they work in areas traditionally called "professions" or in other occupations, they wish to consider their job-related decisions in relation to ethical principles and social goals. They rightly recognize that many, if not most, ethical problems facing all of us arise in our occupational lives: we are often expected to conduct ourselves "at work" in ways which appear to conflict with the ethical principles believed valid in other social relationships; in our occupations themselves certain normally accepted practices sometimes seem to contradict each other; in short, ethical dilemmas of enormous proportion face the morally conscientious person. Whether philosophical ethics can help resolve these acute problems is an inescapable question.

A third recent development is the growing tendency of students to think of themselves as persons who do or will have certain occupational roles. This tendency is noticeable at several stages of life—in choosing an occupation, in preparing for one already chosen, and in pursuing one that has been entered some time ago.

The convergence of these three contemporary developments has created a need for appropriate teaching materials. The *Occupational Ethics* Series is designed to meet this need. Each volume has been written by a philosopher, with the advice or collaboration of a practitioner in a particular occupation. The volumes are suitable for liberal arts courses in ethics and for programs of preprofessional study, as well as for the general reader who seeks a better understanding of a world that most human beings inhabit, the world of work.

John E. Atwell and Elizabeth L. Beardsley, Editors

Preface

Perhaps you have noticed that there are many books on ethical problems in other professions: business ethics, medical ethics, and legal ethics, for example. This book was inspired by those books in an indirect way. Why is it, we asked, that academics seek out and study the ethical problems in other professions and ignore those in their own professions? We thank John Atwell and Elizabeth Beardsley for taking our question seriously. There are many ethical problems in higher education, we said. "Yes," they replied. Academics should write about problems in their own profession, we said. "Yes," they replied. Why, we could even write a whole book about them, we said. "Yes," they replied. So we did.

We canvassed, interviewed, and discussed ethical problems with students, faculty members, and administrators from many institutions to find out what moral issues and dilemmas were important to them. We interviewed scholars at professional meetings, talked with students at a number of schools, and wrote to colleagues across the country, asking for experiences and anecdotes that we could follow up. Our respondents' eagerness and enthusiasm for the project surprised us. Almost everyone had one or several problems to discuss and experiences to share. Many were problems that everyone confronts: unfairness, abuse, exploitation, and conflict of interest. Despite the Ivory Tower Myth, academics are not immune from pettiness and immorality. Dedication to the pursuit of knowledge does no more to ensure morally correct behavior than dedication to the pursuit of wealth. In both cases, power, competition, envy, pressure, insensitivity, and anger promote immoral behavior. However, the world of higher education engenders moral difficulties and dilemmas that manifest themselves in special forms. In this book we have tried to cover ethical problems that are unique to, or characteristic of, higher education because of its goals, structures, and relation to the rest of the world.

We are grateful to the many people at colleges and universities around the country who took our project to heart, talked with and helped us, read our drafts, and contributed ideas. Special thanks to Julie Hooks and Maria Casale, who read early drafts and helped greatly with background research. We thank the other friends and colleagues who read the entire manuscript and gave us comments: Michael Bayles, Esther Carpenter, Jim Henle, Demetra Moulton, John Moulton, Bonnie Robinson, Joe Robinson and Frans van der Bogert. Thank you, Doris Michaels at Prentice-Hall and three conscientious reviewers who gave detailed suggestions for improvements. We thank the members of the Five College Professional Ethics Seminar—Vere Chappell, John Connolly, Mickey Glazer, Murray Kiteley, Joe Marcus, and special guest David Lyons—for a very helpful session on the first draft of Chapter 4. A grant from the Smith College Aid to Faculty Scholarship Committee provided funds for our research assistants and for preparation of the manuscript.

Frederik Pohl and Cyril Kornbluth, when asked of a jointly-authored work "who did what?", are reported to have replied that one of them wrote the nouns and the other the verbs. When we are asked the same question, we answer that one of us wrote the vowels and the other the consonants. This reply represents the spirit of our collaboration on this book; even the smallest meaningful unit was a joint effort. We did everything together and together we take responsibility for it. The order in which our names appear on the cover is the reverse of the order on our previous book and that was determined after a lengthy Alphonse and Gaston routine.

It is usual to thank the secretarial staff who type, retype and proofread a book. Our secretarial staff was the Smith College VAX 11/780 computer. We are very grateful to the director of the Academic Computing Center, Lynn Goodhue, and to her staff, who created a system that is accessible to people in every discipline, easy to learn, and fun to use.

Ethical Problems
In Higher Education

Chapter 1

Introduction:
Ethical Problems
Intrinsic to Higher Education

Most of us who study ethics do so in an academic setting. However, we usually look outside academia for examples and dilemmas to test our principles. We discuss the problems of people in lifeboats deciding between starvation and cannibalism, business executives deciding whether to market a product they think may be dangerous, nurses and doctors deciding how to deal with the terminally ill, and space explorers confronting alien beings with "unearthly" values. Perhaps it gives us some perspective to look at problems from a distance, but there are also advantages to studying what is near at hand. Scholars of ethics have not given much attention to the problems in the very institutions in which most of them work.

THE IVORY TOWER MYTH

The myth that institutions of higher education are sheltered from the struggles and conflicts of the "real world" is widely accepted even by people who ought to know better—those of us in academic settings who confront, struggle with, bemoan, or try to ignore the serious ethical issues that arise. People outside academia may tease us about the ivory tower world and our innocence and naiveté. With a twinge of guilt, we in academia accept their teasing because the myth tells us that we are a privileged lot, protected as others are not. Naive? Perhaps, we think, but isn't it nice that we don't have to get our ethical feet dirty in the moral slime outside our refuge. There is great comfort in the myth. We may be naive, but we do not have to worry about being evil.

One purpose of this book is to dispel this myth. There are many benefits of higher education, but immunity from ethical problems is not one of them. Pretending that ethical problems do not exist is not unique to academia, but the Ivory Tower Myth has elevated this self-deception to policy so that serious study of the ethical issues in higher education has largely been ignored. Two exceptions are Pierre Van den Berghe's (1970) charming satire *Academic Gamesmanship* and Derek Bok's (1982) *Beyond the Ivory*

1

Tower about the relation of university administration to government and large donors.

Many people are directly involved in the ethical conflicts in academic institutions: students, faculty members, administrators, staff members, and trustees. There are also people outside the institution who have important roles in its operation: legislators, officials of granting agencies, endowers, and parents of students. In this chapter we give a brief overview of the types of ethical problems that arise for people who study and work in institutions of higher education along with some main themes that recur in different areas. In later chapters we detail some of these problems.

INHERENT MORAL CONFLICTS

Some moral dilemmas arise from the varied goals and functions of academic institutions. For example, students may have moral concerns in choosing courses and fields of study, in choosing between the informal social education of college life and the formal education and study that college provides, and sometimes in choosing between learning and the acquisition of credentials, which are the ticket to jobs, further education, and other opportunities.

There are moral conflicts between fund raising and maintaining educational quality, between benefiting the public at large and benefiting the people who work in the institutions, and between the goal of quality sought by the evaluation process and the well-being and happiness of those who are evaluated.

There are problems for granting agencies, researchers, and librarians, who fund, perform, and support the activities of learning and research and who can use their power to control what is taught and the development and distribution of new knowledge. And because they have different goals, perspectives, and backgrounds, moral conflicts can arise between administrators, faculty, students, and staff.

Moral conflicts are exacerbated when an institution faces economic difficulties. Decisions on how funds and benefits are to be allocated and which areas of study will receive encouraging support are constrained by financial considerations, increasing the potential for injustice. Staff cutbacks increase the conflict between teaching and research. Faculty members are asked to do more teaching and at the same time are pressured to increase research that attracts outside funds to help support the institution. Students find that economic and academic considerations are in competition. Loans and scholarships vanish, outside employment cuts into study time, and worry about getting jobs makes grades more important than learning. Economic concerns increase the temptation to cut corners and violate ethical principles.

Scarce resources put pressure on academic institutions to find additional sources of funding. Aggressive fund raising can create moral problems such as misrepresentation of the potential benefits of contributions, investment in corporations or countries that offer high yields but whose products or policies may be morally reprehensible, acceptance of contributions that carry conditions either overtly or in the form of secret agreements, and research contracts with corporations and government agencies that involve violation of principles the institution would otherwise uphold.

Some institutions of higher education compete with each other for the best students, whereas others compete for enough students to meet budgetary demands. As a result they may exaggerate or misrepresent their strengths and benefits to incoming students. For example, they may mislead prospective students about their faculty/student ratio, their scholarship opportunities, and their educational resources. (In this book we provide examples and problems boxed off from the text. Here is one now.)

When toothpaste, automobile, and soap ads tell us that using their products will improve our sex lives, we may groan cynically. But do we apply the same critical scrutiny to the promises of educational institutions? Just as a toothpaste company may spend millions on a thirty-second television commercial to sell its product, some colleges and universities invest large amounts of money in a winning football team, support of sororities and fraternities, and the production of brochures and catalogs with pictures of happy young people on a lovely campus in order to secure funds and students. When we shop for a used car or house, we do not expect the sellers to tell us about the faults of their products. We learn the principles of "buyer beware" and do not think it particularly unethical if the seller fails to point out the flaws we have overlooked. When a university advertises the cultural advantages and excitement of its location in a big city but fails to mention the pollution, crime, and surrounding slums, does the same principle operate? Or do we expect something different from an institution of higher education? Should we?

Most academic institutions are devoted both to passing on knowledge—the aim of teaching—and to the creation of new knowledge—the aim of research. Students are the immediate beneficiaries of teaching. Student beneficiaries are real and immediate. The beneficiaries of research are usually more abstract and less immediate: the fund of knowledge of the species, society as a whole, or the particular field of study. Research may add to the prestige of the particular institution and advance the career of the individual researcher. Only rarely are the consequential benefits of research immediate and profound. Occasionally the results of research may even be harmful. However, for many reasons, most academic institutions value research more highly than teaching. The problem of which goal to pursue—

teaching or research—falls most heavily on the individual faculty member, who is supposed to do both and has to divide limited time and energy between the two. But it is also a serious problem for administrators, legislators, and anyone else who has the means of influencing the goals of the institution.

In the teaching realm there are deep ethical questions involved in deciding who to educate and what that education should be. With limited facilities, should an institution provide higher-quality education for relatively few people or lower-quality education for a greater number? How are these people to be selected? Should the criterion be academic ability alone or should other criteria, such as educational need or diversity of the student body, be considered? Has the world changed so that a college education, like a high school education, should be a right that is available to everyone? What proportion of educational effort should go into compensatory and remedial programs? Should teachers aim at the brightest and most advanced student in the class, at the average student, or at the student with the least ability and preparation? How should a college curriculum balance vocationally relevant training with exposure to the richness and diversity of different arts and cultures that may have few vocational advantages?

Teachers have considerable influence and power over their students. The asymmetry of power in student-faculty relations can lead to ethical problems ranging from indentured servitude to sexual harassment. Faculty members select the course material and approaches with which students work. The biases of professors may involve important ethical considerations for a wide range of courses, from political science to computer science. One recurring question in these issues is the fact-value problem: Can one ever separate the "facts" from the value-laden perspectives and contexts that contain them?

Evaluation is a central function in an academic institutions; it is a part of nearly everything done at the institution. Students and their work are evaluated by the faculty; faculty members and administrators evaluate other faculty members; both students and faculty members evaluate research; and now students also evaluate faculty members. The resulting decisions affect the character and quality of knowledge and the distribution of authority and power. Evaluation raises a number of interesting ethical problems: How does the evaluation system help or hurt people and help or hurt the goals of the institution? What criteria are used in the evaluation? Who should do the evaluating? Can or should people outside the institution (possibly the courts) have any role in these evaluations and the appeals from them? To what extent can the evaluation be objective, or do the values of those doing the evaluating always affect their judgments?

Another set of ethical problem areas for higher education involves the concepts of honesty, fairness, and the reward system. Cheating, dishonesty in research, and plagiarism are complex notions. They often depend on the conventions of particular fields and particular times, blurring the borderline between right and wrong. Many of these issues are closely tied to the reward systems that influence the people who work in institutions of higher education. Students learn how to modify their behavior to get higher grades; faculty members learn how to increase their chances for promotion, job security, and recognition; administrators learn how to manage departments and institutions so as to minimize friction and expenditures, how to court potential contributors, and increase donations.

The issues in the ethics of higher education are related to more general ethical and philosophical questions. We shall provide a framework for our particular concerns by outlining these more general topics briefly. First we look at how ethical theories relate to moral problems and decisions and consider the similarities and differences between ethical theories and scientific theories. Next we describe some major principles that are prominent in ethical theory. Then we discuss a problem in the application of ethical theory: the relation between facts and values.

This book can be read without any additional background in ethical theory. The reader who wants more information about ethical theories can look at some of the classic theories such as Aristotle's *Nichomachean Ethics,* Plato's *Republic,* Hume's *Treatise on Human Nature* and *Enquiry Concerning the Principles of Morals,* Mill's *Utilitarianism,* and Kant's *Groundwork for the Metaphysics of Morals* and *Critique of Practical Reason.* Introductory level textbooks such as Frankena's *Ethics* (1963), Frankena and Granrose's *Introductory Readings in Ethics* (1974), Singer's *Practical Ethics* (1979) and Wolff's *Introductory Philosophy* (1979) explain a wide range of ethical views clearly. They are also valuable for their suggestions for further readings.

ETHICAL THEORIES

Our purpose is to present some of the moral issues in higher education. We are not going to solve many moral problems; rather, we shall highlight some of them and explain what the issues are. Explanations of why something is morally right or wrong can vary enormously. They may invoke the concepts of justice, freedom, equality, rights, duties and obligations, or the Principle of Maximizing Benefits. They may consider what would happen if particular practices became common or universal. They may depend on the principle of treating rational agents as ends in themselves, not merely as means. There are principles of fairness and equal opportunity. There is conflict between democracy and meritocracy: When should benefits be available to everyone and when should ability, potential, and achievement influence the distribution of benefits and opportunities? There are problems that involve rules and precedents and how they are applied and interpreted and, of course, problems that involve weighing the costs and benefits of some policy or procedure in comparison with what is involved in carrying it out.

Although ethical theories help clarify what is involved in a moral issue, they rarely tell us what to do in a particular moral dilemma. They focus on principles rather than conclusions and on reasoning rather than outcomes. How, then, do they contribute to the understanding of ethical issues?

We can compare ethical theories with scientific theories. There are some differences: Scientific theories explain how things are and ethical theories explain how things ought to be; scientific reasoning is called *explanation* and ethical reasoning is called *justification*. The data and explanations in science often can be appreciated fully only by a specialist. In ethics we are all supposed to be able to appreciate the data and reasoning of ethical justifications. However, the similarities between scientific and ethical theories help us understand the status of ethical theories in a discussion of moral problems. Let us look at some of the properties of scientific and ethical theories:

1. Scientific theories are abstractions or claims about what the basic principles or properties of the phenomena are. Similarly, ethical theories focus on the basic principles or properties of ethical phenomena. For example, justifications in terms of fairness, equality, the Golden Rule, or maximizing benefits represent attempts to account for the huge variety of moral issues in terms of a limited number of basic features.

2. There is a complex relation between scientific theory and specific cases. If a single case conflicts with a theory, that case is often set aside, ignored, or considered a technical difficulty. Adjustments and modifications may be made to a theory to help it cover the problem case. Rarely is a theory given up because of problem cases. This is also the case in ethics, where adherents of a theory treat apparent counterexamples as scientists do. For example, there are situations where sacrificing someone as a scapegoat may actually maximize benefits but this seems so unfair that it is morally repugnant. Therefore, theories that advocate maximizing benefits will either defend the scapegoat sacrifice or show that it would not actually maximize benefits in the long run. But the theory is not abandoned.

3. A scientific theory may provide an explanation without predicting exactly what will happen. Newton's laws can never tell us the final destination of a particular boulder in a landslide, although they can explain what forces are involved. Similarly, an ethical theory may not tell us just what to do, but it will indicate what principles are involved.

4. Different scientific theories may present different views of the world. Different theories may offer different descriptions of the facts. Even if they can agree on the facts, they may disagree about how to explain them. Thus, disputes between theories cannot always be decided by further observation alone. Very often the main disagreements between theories are

disagreements about which basic properties and principles should be used to give an explanation. The same is true for ethical theories.

Different ethical theories, principles and beliefs are likely to provide different justifications for the problems we are going to discuss. Ethical theories are not concerned only with what is right and wrong but more with *why*, explaining what principles are involved and what alternative explanations are possible. They also help us make explicit our own personal ethical theories: the principles and guidelines we use to make our own ethical decisions and judgments.

In this book we refer regularly to a core set of general ethical principles that are used to determine the morality of actions and are employed by several major theories. Here they are.

1. *The Principle of Fairness.* Persons who are equal in aspects relevant to a particular situation should receive equal treatment. Most of the problems involved in applying this principle concern decisions about which aspects *are* relevant. How do we decide what counts as equal treatment, what rights are involved, how justice is to be realized, and what people deserve? In fact, the Principle of Fairness does not say by itself what sort of distribution *is* fair or what counts as equal treatment. We recognize different systems in different situations. For example, distribution of benefits (medical care) in an emergency room is done on the basis of need rather than ability or accomplishment. In other cases accomplishments alone form the basis for reward; in still others potential or ability is important. Other principles must be invoked to determine what sort of distribution is fair.

2. *The Principle of Maximizing Benefits.* Most problems encountered in applying this principle involve weighing the costs and benefits of an act and deciding the scope of application of the principle: Who should be considered—the people in the situation, those outside who may be affected, animals, future generations? What is to count as a benefit—the creation of happiness, the realization of higher goals, the future of the species? The other area of difficulty involves decisions about how to distribute benefits. Benefits can be maximized, but this still leaves the question of how much each person gets. For example, one may argue that maximizing the benefits of higher education requires that it be limited to the academically talented and therefore not be given to everyone. Providing higher education for everyone would lessen the total amount of benefits produced. (We consider this claim in Chapters 2 and 5.) These decisions are under the control of the Principle of Fairness.

The Principle of Maximizing Benefits can conflict with the Principle of Fairness. In some cases benefits might be maximized by treating one person or group unfairly, denying them benefits so that others can have more. Different ethical theories disagree about which principle, if either, should take precedence in such cases.

3. *The Principle of Universalization.* What would happen if everyone did it? This principle is related to the first two principles we have discussed. Universalization is related to the moral problems of setting precedents. When one person does something, others may want to do it too, and then everyone in a similar position should be able to. If one person benefits, other people should be able to benefit also. It employs the same notion of impartiality that the Principle of Fairness uses. Morality should apply to everyone impartially. It is not right to favor particular people in the application of moral principles. To apply this principle, one must find the aspects of a situation that are relevant for the generalization. There are different ways of describing any act or situation. What would happen if everyone did *what?* An interesting problem with this principle is that some acts may be outside its scope, some things "everybody" would not want or be able to do. This principle seems to rule out actions that would be disastrous *if* everyone did them but which are not otherwise immoral and which not everyone would want to do.

The Principle of Universalization is usually applied when an act is generalized very broadly, considering the consequences if everyone (or at least many people) in the relevant situation were to do the act. There are related principles that consider the consequences if an act were to be generalized more narrowly to a single other person or group. The Principle of Reciprocity and the Golden Rule are examples. These generalization principles ask us to consider what it would be like if someone does to us what we plan to do to them.

4. *The Principle of Treating Others as Ends in Themselves, Not Merely as Means.* This principle entails treating others with respect and dignity and recognizing that they have desires and plans that should be considered. This principle is also related to the others we have examined. One has to consider the interests of other people involved and not just oneself when making moral decisions. In effect, this principle requires that we not exploit others and that we consider both sides in conflict situations, but it does not, by itself, tell us what to do.

In our description of the four principles we pointed out some of their commonalities. Some of the principles look at the consequences of an action (maximizing benefits or setting precedents) in order to judge its morality. Other principles evaluate an action on its own merits (its fairness or its intention to treat others as ends in themselves). In many applications the four principles converge on the same solution to an ethical problem. This also happens with scientific theories, where more than one theory may lead to the same prediction. On the other hand, applying scientific theories is often most interesting where two or more theories conflict. This is also true for ethical theories. Interesting cases occur where the four principles we have described conflict and lead to different ethical decisions.

THE RELATION BETWEEN FACTS
AND VALUES

It may seem that facts, along with knowledge and truth, are by themselves neither right nor wrong. Rightness and wrongness are values, and facts are distinct from values. In this view facts are ethically neutral. At first look the distinction is attractive. It explains why there seems to be more disagreement on moral judgments than on other kinds of judgments. Facts are objective, independent of personal viewpoint, and independently knowable, but the values placed on facts, which form the basis for moral judgments, are subjective, or dependent on the individual viewpoint.

However, with a closer look the distinction becomes blurry. Not only are there frequent disagreements about factual descriptions, it is not clear that factual descriptions can ever be completely separated from values. The facts we seek are motivated by the values we have. The descriptions of those facts depend on the things that are important to us. The way we categorize and classify things and events is based on our personal knowledge and values (Kuhn 1962; Harding and Hintikka 1983).

Creatures that live off other creatures without contributing anything in return are called parasites, and by extension we apply the term and its exploitative sense to some humans who do the same thing. But infants and others whose dependence is accepted are not called parasites. Categories are determined by the values of the people doing the categorizing. The distinctions we make in "factual" descriptions reflect our values, and some of those values are ethical values.

We are encouraged to consider alcoholism a disease beyond the control of the victim because alcoholics are more likely to stop drinking if given sympathy instead of blame. Poverty is often thought to be a responsibility of society rather than a disease or a blameworthy plight. In both cases our classification is determined by what we think is the best remedy and by our belief that these situations are undesirable. How would we classify poverty if it were considered a desirable condition, a choice of will or vocation, and a state of purity? Would it be possible for alcoholism to be classified as a special ability or a blessing by another culture?

Even very abstract values can affect the way facts are gathered and applied. For example, it has frequently been assumed that scientific theories can be evaluated by criteria that are themselves neutral. One of these criteria is generality: The more general a scientific claim, the more valuable it is.

This criterion encourages the search for unifying principles. But when carelessly applied, the criterion of generality can mislead the direction of research and even lead to harmful applications. Much research on sex differences in human intelligence and behavior attempts to discover the extent to which differences are innate rather than "merely" the result of cultural differences in the treatment of males and females. The "impartial" standard of generality favors innateness, independently of any evidence for it, merely because it is more general—part of the genetic endowment of the entire species and not merely a particular feature of one of many diverse human cultures. Claims that sex differences are innate have ethical implications for the way males and females are treated in the society.

Is there no area of study that is free of ethical significance? Study of the past may seem ethically harmless, even though ethical judgments are made in deciding what to report and what to ignore. But the major ethical import of history is likely to be its application. Historical accounts ennoble some events and peoples and disparage or ignore others. Because history gives us pictures about the world, about what was right or wrong, worthwhile or fruitless, and leaves us with lessons and views that guide our behavior, it has important ethical consequences. Like history, other fields have ethical implications. Mathematics seems abstract enough to have no ethical significance, but mathematics serves as a crucial tool for other studies. For example, it is used to predict population rates, nuclear survival potential, and the feasibility of complex computer designs in medicine, weaponry, and transportation. In many cases the use of the studies and their ethical import, whether in history, mathematics, philosophy, or computer science, are not remote and indirect but closely connected to the purpose of the study.

Even though values are involved in all descriptions of facts, this does not mean that descriptions of facts are arbitrary or incorrect. However, it does mean that attempts to be neutral, to seek knowledge for its own sake and avoid moral dilemmas, may not be easy or even possible.

In the following chapters we apply ethical concepts to problems in higher education. First we look at the academic institution and its relation to society. Then we examine some of the problems of colleges and universities in relation to the people who work and study in them. Next we look at ethical problems that arise in the two main activities of the educational institution: research and teaching. Finally we summarize our brief study, highlighting the common themes.

SUMMARY

There is a myth that ethical problems do not occur in institutions of higher education. Although a pleasant fiction, this is far from true. Moral conflicts and problems arise in every aspect of higher education and are exacerbated when economic difficulties, declining enrollment, outside pressures, and changes in interests occur. The relation between the institution and the outside world, the power structure, evaluation, and reward systems within academia, create possibilities for unethical behavior.

We first examine the role of ethical theories in the discussion of moral issues. An ethical theory, like a scientific theory, represents an attempt to explain different sorts of moral situations in terms of a limited number of principles. We introduce the principles of Fairness, Maximizing Benefits, Universalization, and Treating Others as Ends in Themselves. We argue that no area of study in higher education involves "pure" facts, that every area assumes, invokes, and uses values that have ethical significance.

Chapter 2

The Academic Institution
and its Relation
to Society

In this chapter we discuss some of the ethical problems facing administrators and others who determine the role and structure of academic institutions and control their daily workings. Administrative decisions sometimes hurt individuals or groups or put them at a disadvantage, but like many things that cause pain they may be ethically justified. This is true at all levels of higher education. Although voting to deny someone tenure or discontinuing an unpopular or financially unsuccessful program causes pain, it may be irresponsible or unfair to students, faculty, and the whole school not to make such painful judgments. Administrators are often faced with conflicts between what is advantageous and what is right for other people, for their own institutions, for higher education in general, or for the larger society.

There are many different types of institutions of higher education: two-year junior colleges, community colleges, privately endowed colleges and universities, state colleges and universities, military academies, seminaries for religious studies, professional schools (law, medicine, nursing, etc.), and postdoctoral institutes for advanced study. Despite their differences, they all have in common the pursuit of knowledge: the discovery, organization, and passing on of knowledge. Are there times when the academic goals of these institutions clash with moral values?

We first look at the relation between moral values and these academic goals. Are academic values independent of, and sometimes in conflict with, ethical goals? The relation of academic institutions to the rest of the world raises the question of the purpose of knowledge. To what extent is knowledge valued as a means to some further end, such as practical benefits for humankind, and to what extent is it valued for its own sake?

We then consider some of the ways academic institutions interact with the outside world. We analyze reasons for academic neutrality in ethical and political conflicts and describe how academic institutions affect local communities. Next we discuss some aspects of the financial structure and support of educational institutions: the exploitation of some academic and nonacademic workers in order to provide more resources for a few, the pros and cons of unionization, pandering for outside donations, and support for military research. Finally, we consider the institution's responsibilities to students and its role in guiding and controlling their lives and values.

ETHICAL PRINCIPLES
AND ACADEMIC VALUES

The ethical principles described in Chapter 1 encourage people to promote fairness, equal opportunity, justice, and individual freedom; avoid hurting others; help the less fortunate; set good examples; and not treat others only as means toward one's own ends. In terms of moral values a better world is one in which people are fairer, more just, and more considerate of other people's interests.

Academic values seem to be different. They promote the discovery and exchange of knowledge and ideas. In terms of academic values a better world is one where people are wiser, more knowledgeable, and more intellectually resourceful. The activities that go on in academic institutions are supposed to serve these goals. For example, decisions on hiring, firing, promotion, and grading are supposed to be made on bases that advance knowledge, independent of whether the outcomes hurt individuals, limit freedom, or reduce opportunities. There are times when the goals of an academic institution seem to be in direct conflict with ethical principles. Sometimes it appears that we have to decide whether to do something that is justified from an academic standpoint but not from a moral standpoint.

Here are some questions raised by academics we have interviewed. Should we lie about the advantages of our school if that will help attract better students, faculty, and funding? (One college president told us that lying is a necessary part of the job.) Should ethical misconduct be overlooked if the transgressor is an outstanding scholar? Should the salaries of the faculty be increased at the expense of the salaries of secretaries and the support staff? How do we reconcile conflicting feelings of admiration and hatred for a very clever but evil person (for example, a person who brilliantly defends a political policy we abhor)?

How are academic and moral values related? There are three main possibilities to consider: that academic values may be dependent on, or justified by, moral values; that academic values and moral values may be independent and equal; or that academic values and moral values may be independent, with moral values superior.

There are other possibilities: that moral values are inferior to or justified by academic values. A version of this view has been argued by claiming that rationality is what makes morality possible and that consistency is the ultimate test of moral rightness (compare Kant's views). But let us consider only the three main possibilities.

How might moral principles be used to justify academic values? The benefits and power of higher education are denied to many people. Academic rewards and opportunity are not given out on the basis of need or moral worth, but rather on the basis of accomplishment or promise.

In the United States, every citizen is guaranteed twelve years of education. In fact, most of those years are compulsory. However, higher education is reserved only for a talented minority of citizens since admission to college is highly competitive. Education up to college is thought to be a right, but after that it is considered a privilege. Why this difference? How does this fit with the ideals of fairness and equal opportunity?

One defense of reserving higher education for the talented is that everyone will gain the most in the long run, that is to say, freedom and justice and other moral values will be served best if the limited academic resources are restricted to those who are most qualified to use them. This defense depends on the Principle of Maximizing Benefits. In order for this defense to work, it must be true that concentrating educational resources on a talented few really does produce more benefits. It is possible that using educational resources to maximize literacy, informed judgments, appreciation and understanding of academic subjects by *all* citizens would result in greater benefits even though knowledge might advance more slowly. If this were true, academic practices that are optimal for achieving academic goals might not be morally justifiable on the grounds of maximizing benefits.

One can try to give a moral justification for such academic practices by considering them a kind of contract or promise. Once the arrangement is set up and publicly recognized and once expectations are created, it would be wrong to violate the conditions of the contract. The smooth running of a complex society requires that such contracts be depended on. We cannot violate the conditions of the "academic evaluation contract" because doing so would serve as a precedent for violating other contracts. If violating contracts became general practice, no one would be able to depend on prior agreements or conventions and society would fall apart.

Although this argument based on social stability has force, it presumes that the practices required by the contract are morally worthwhile to begin with. Some social customs that we learn to expect, which can even be called implicit contracts, are immoral nonetheless. For example, everyone may think that sellers of used cars lie about the condition of their cars or that racial or religious bigotry is common, and many things would have to change if these practices suddenly stopped. Laws protecting consumers would become unnecessary, leaving consumer protection agencies with nothing to do and people who had grown to expect dishonestly or bigotry would become confused and suspicious. But such disruptions of the social order do *not* mean that dishonesty or bigotry should continue. Thus, it is not enough to show that academic practices constitute a sort of agreement, a convention that would cause some social discomfort if it were given up. One has to show that academic practices that seem to conflict with ethical principles are actually morally worthwhile.

We think it fair that academic rewards are distributed to those who deserve them, but how is this decided? Current members of the academic community control the decisions. The tests used to evaluate ability and promise are designed by academics. The criteria for graduation, promotion and academic honors are chosen by the academic community. We take for granted that the best judges of who deserves what are those who are already experts in the system: the current members of the academy. Compare this with the political realm, where the ethical ideal is the democratic election procedure. Power and prestige are bestowed on those elected to office by citizens who are not politicians themselves. The evaluation of merit is determined not by experts in politics but by the people who are affected by this power. Is the political sphere so different from the academic that different procedures should be used to decide who deserves what? If not, does this mean that the method of evaluating merit should be changed in one case? Which one?

We may think that current academic *practices* do not produce the greatest benefits, and do not maximize justice, freedom, or other moral values, but still believe that academic values are worthwhile and morally justifiable. Current academic practices may not be the best ones for fostering academic values. Better institutions and structures might be possible in which academic and moral values would more often agree. If this is the case, we should consider which ethical principles would be most successful in defending academic values. Should academic values be designed to maximize benefits? Can we use the Principle of Universalization to consider alternatives? What if everyone were to go to college? To do research? To have the authority and prestige of an academic?

We may want to conclude that academic values are not justified by moral values. The pursuit of knowledge is good in its own right. Then how are the two values to be compared? What happens when there is a conflict?

Our second alternative is that academic and moral values are independent. But if this is the case, we may have a conflict if they tell us to do different things. If one set of values does not clearly take precedence over the other, in other words if they have equal status, then irreconcilable conflicts may arise between them. And this raises the possibility that something that is academically justified may not be morally justified.

If academic values have equal status with moral values, there may be no reason to choose the morally best action rather than the academically best one. In order to capture our feeling that immoral actions should *not* be done even if they are justifiable on other grounds, some ethical theories hold the third alternative: that moral values take precedence over all other values. The value of knowledge for its own sake, or for some other non-moral benefit would be a lesser value. In this view, conflicts between academic and moral values are not irreconcilable. Whichever course of action would best promote the moral values is the correct one.

However, this view does not explain why academic values sometimes appear to take precedence over moral values. For example, we do not think it wrong to award Nobel prizes in physics to the people who make the most outstanding intellectual contributions in this field rather than to the physicists who lead the most exemplary lives. Sometimes it seems more appropriate to uphold academic standards than to reduce pain and suffering or maximize equal opportunity. For example, we do not think it wrong that students who fail to do passing work should receive a failing grade even though failure may hurt the student to such an extent that it outweighs the benefits of teaching the student a lesson and saving the world from incompetent graduates.

Since these actions do not seem immoral, perhaps we should look again at the possibility that academic values, and those academic practices that actually promote academic values, do have a moral justification after all.

KNOWLEDGE AS A MEANS
OR AN END

Considering the relation of moral and academic values raises a central question about academic values: Is knowledge valuable for its own sake or only as a means to some other end? Should students be prepared for a vocation, that is, trained as practitioners in particular fields, or should they be educated broadly, regardless of whether the knowledge has clear applications? Should research always be in the service of particular problems, social needs, or technological advances, or should research problems be chosen because they are interesting in their own right regardless of whether they contribute to some other end? Is knowledge valuable only when it is useful?

Earlier we considered the possibility that distributing educational resources to everyone might lessen the total gain in knowledge and wisdom. According to this position, restricting higher education to the most talented is the best way to maximize benefits. However, if we wish to be sure of maximizing benefits, it seems that academic institutions have a moral obligation to concentrate on more popular or practical problems. Under these conditions it may be *immoral* to divert academic resources into esoteric areas that are not likely to yield practical benefits.

Some people argue that important research breakthroughs of practical importance have occurred when researchers worked on problems that had no known application at the time. Therefore, it *will* provide more benefits in the long run if researchers are encouraged to work on any area that seems interesting to them, regardless of its known applications. This argument is persuasive in mathematics and the sciences, where abstract problems have been worked on for their own sake and later have been found to have practical applications. However, in some areas of study, benefits to nonacademics are so unlikely that this argument does not work. Classicists and musicologists study subjects that may be of great interest and importance to other classicists and musicologists but are very unlikely to benefit nonacademics. Should research in these areas be stopped or given low priority?

There is a tendency for academics to associate vocationally relevant study and applied research with intellectual shallowness. However unfair this association may be, it has the effect of giving purely theoretical study a heightened status. Thus, by having no application or vocational use and no interest to those outside academia, purely theoretical study has been assumed to be interesting and more intellectually deep and demanding. This contempt for nonacademic interests is derived at least partly from resentment of the control they can have over academic pursuits. But it is also a form of academic snobbery, scorning the concerns of outsiders. It can have ethical repercussions if it leads scholars to avoid research *because* the research is useful or important to the nonacademic world.

Is it a form of prostitution for an academic to work on intellectually less interesting problems because they are generously funded by outside agencies? What is the difference?

NEUTRALITY IN ETHICAL ISSUES

Now that we have looked at the possibility that academic values and goals may conflict with moral values, let us look at how academic institutions treat outside ethical and political conflicts. Because of the respect they gain from their role as specialists in knowledge, academic institutions have considerable influence on the rest of the world. But colleges and universities usually *avoid* official stands in political controversies, trying to remain neutral. This general policy may be an attempt to protect academic freedom, to say in effect that we shall leave politics alone if it leaves us alone. It may also represent a recognition that the opinions of experts, even in another field, can be inappropriately persuasive. Most academics may have no better judgment than anyone else about ethical and political questions, but their status as academics tends to give their opinions extra weight. We may be treating others only as means if we impose our moral views on them by using the force of academic authority to persuade unfairly. On the other hand, it seems immoral never to take a stand or not even try to change the conditions of an immoral situation. The Principle of Universalization would suggest that a policy of always avoiding moral issues, of never taking a stand, would be wrong.

However, even in controversial cases where the morally right action is not clear, it is sometimes impossible for an institution with power and influence to be neutral since doing nothing in a political crisis constitutes a kind of action. Such default actions by a school may be *indirect* political statements.

Richard Nixon, after resigning the presidency under threat of impeachment, offered his presidential papers to Duke University, where he attended law school. Usually it would be an honor for a school to receive the documents of a President, but in this case many faculty members felt that accepting the papers would constitute approval of Nixon's behavior in office. After considerable controversy, Duke accepted the papers. Was Duke taking a political stand by agreeing to be the home of the Nixon presidential library?

Smith College invited UN Ambassador Jeanne Kirkpatrick, an outspoken defender of Ronald Reagan's controversial policies in El Salvador, to be its commencement speaker and receive an honorary degree. Many faculty members and students objected to the invitation. They did not object to her speaking on campus, but they argued that by inviting her to speak on a special occasion and bestowing an honorary degree, Smith College was expressing political approval of her views and of American policies in El Salvador. Were they correct? Do such invitations and awards constitute endorsements of policies?

Some of the strongest criticism about the indirect political activity of academic institutions has been aimed at their financial investments. Just as it would be immoral for colleges and universities to finance assassinations or the deliberate dumping of toxic wastes, critics argue that they should not support governments with racist laws or companies that pollute the environment. Investments that help maintain the economy of a company or government help maintain its policies and practices, thus violating the independent neutrality of the institution of higher education. Withdrawing funds from existing investments is as much a political statement as refusing to invest. This issue became salient during the Vietnamese War, when many argued that colleges and universities *should* take a stand against the way by divesting themselves of stock in domestic corporations that manufacture war materiel.

The moral and academic values of an institution come into direct conflict when investment in a morally questionable state or corporation yields high profits. Colleges and universities that are having trouble meeting their budget obligations find divestment of a profitable stock very difficult. The institution is firmly committed to carrying out its educational mission, and the money from morally dubious investments is put to use maintaining and improving the educational resources of the institution.

Arguments for maintaining such investments are of two kinds. The first claims that academic values are as important to maintain as moral and political values. The academy has a duty to maintain them at the highest level possible even if this means sacrificing some moral sensitivity and political improvements in order to do so. This is an "ends justify the means" argument.

The second argument claims that even if we consider the moral and political values to be more important, the results of maintaining academic values—a populace with better judgment and more knowledge—will result in the *eventual* improvement of moral and political life. This is an "it is moral in the long run" argument. Both views imply that apparently immoral means are justified by superior ends.

Why are such arguments suspect? In order to be effective they must at least show that the immorality of the means is slight compared with the benefits of the ends, but these differences may be hard to measure. How do we measure the consequences of withdrawing investments? The Principle of Universalization suggests that divestment would be good if it set a precedent for other investors. But would it? How do we decide whether a divestment action represents a justified boycott or an unfair blacklist? The Principle of Maximizing Benefits allows that causing harm and misery is justified if the resulting well-being and happiness are greater. However, if the harm affects only some people and the benefits affect others, the Principle of Fairness and the Principle of Not Using People Only as Means may be violated. For example, one cannot justify financing the oppression of South African blacks merely by citing the benefits to American college students.

One might argue that a single school's withdrawing of its investment will have no significant affect on the company or government in question. But individuals and organizations may have an obligation to express moral disapproval even though such disapproval will not by itself change the situation. When the investment is crucial to the financial health of the school, the issue becomes harder to decide. Defenders of morally suspect investments have argued that the harm done to a school by divestment exceeds the moral gain of merely going on record with an ineffective protest. They claim that while it may be morally honorable to protest, the hardships created keep the action from being morally required.

COMMUNITY RELATIONS

Financial decisions of colleges and universities may not have as great an effect on the world situation as we would like, but they do have a significant impact on the communities in which the institutions are located. Sometimes the academic values that guide the mission of an institution conflict with moral values in its day-to-day business with its neighbors. The effect of the institution on the community is an important one. Institution-centered actions that ignore harm done to those outside the institution are as likely to be immoral as the self-centered actions of individuals.

Because educational institutions are tax-exempt, they use the resources of the local community—for example, roads, and fire and police protection—without directly paying for them. Some schools make sizable voluntary donations to the community in lieu of taxes. Many colleges and universities feel a responsibility to use their resources to help the people in the community as well as the people belonging to the institution. They often open the resources of their libraries, athletic facilities, and cultural facilities to members of the community. Sometimes they provide consultants and volunteers for community problems and projects. Colleges that draw students primarily from the local area—community and city colleges and some small liberal arts colleges—feel a special obligation to serve the community.

Are the voluntary contributions of an institution to its community morally right or not? Our judgments about right and wrong are usually inextricably related to our judgments about the motives and intentions of the people involved. But moral judgments that we can easily make about individuals are sometimes difficult or impossible to make about a larger entity. If individuals do something that appears generous or helpful purely out of self-interest, we may conclude that their deeds are not morally good even though they have beneficial effects. However, it is harder to assign motives to a collective institution, and so it is more difficult to evaluate its actions. There is rarely a single motive behind the good deeds of an academic institution. It is possible that some individuals in the administration promote an action thinking only of themselves or of the institution, and that other individuals promote the action because they believe it is the right thing.

> Frequently the athletic facilities and auditoriums of a college are used by the local community for high school sporting events, town meetings, and concerts. Should colleges feel an obligation to provide these or other services to the community? Do local businesses have the same obligation? What differences might there be between a college and a business in this respect?

The presence of a college or university can dominate a small town or a city neighborhood. The relation of the institution to the town and its people sometimes resembles that of the medieval nobility to their serfs and servants. With many depending on the institution for their livelihoods and most depending on it for the quality of life in the area, local residents may feel pride and gratitude or resentment and jealousy. In many areas the institution attracts people who like the cultural activities and the academic residents. It becomes a desirable place to live for middle-class professionals, former students, artists, and writers. This may improve real estate values, attract new business, and raise the quality of life. There may be negative effects as well. Poorer residents may be driven out as developers convert old residences for higher rents or profitable sales, or there may be an increase in the noise level, drug traffic, vandalism, and drunk driving as a result of student parties.

> Older colleges and universities in large cities are likely to find themselves in poor, deteriorating neighborhoods with high crime rates. The approaches taken to this situation vary. One private university in a large city bought the surrounding poverty and evicted the residents in order to provide housing for its faculty. A public university in another large city bought the surrounding property and subsidized quality low-cost housing in order to keep the neighborhood friendly. A third university simply razed existing housing and turned the surrounding area into parks and lawns, forcing the former residents to move farther away from the university. Does the financial success of these undertakings or the financial need of the university affect our judgment of their morality?

American colleges and universities fill a noneducational role in the economic and social structure of society. By taking 10 million young people out of the job market for four or more years of their lives, colleges and universities provide a buffer for unemployment. With financial support from parents, scholarships, and loans, most students live as marginal consumers and unemployed or part-time minimum wage earners. Without colleges and universities, these millions of young people would go directly from high school to the job market with expectations of independence and decent wages. When the economy is not good, this situation can easily produce demands and unrest that threaten political stability. Therefore, academic institutions provide stability to the economic system by absorbing potential workers. If the economic system is immoral, academic institutions participate in this immorality. Just as financial investments that support immoral organizations deserve moral scrutiny, so other forms of support may also be questioned. When academic institutions claim that they are completely neutral on political issues, this claim ignores their support of the status quo and the incumbent powers.

Many colleges and universities have expanded their continuing education programs in recent years, and many older women are entering such programs as a result of the women's movement. Some women return to school to increase their job skills, but for many the return to school is a way of obtaining a more intellectually stimulating life. The effect may be to leave women less dissatisfied with their lot without actually changing the power structures and conditions of unequal pay that handicap women. Can we decide whether this effect of continuing education programs is morally good or bad?

CONTROL AND SUPPORT OF HIGHER EDUCATION

Within the Institution

As major employers in towns and small cities, many colleges and universities are in a position to exploit their employees. Students who need money may be paid the minimum wage or less for work that requires considerable ability because the supply of needy students is greater than the number of jobs available. Spouses of graduate students and faculty members are routinely hired as secretaries, laboratory technicians, and other staff workers at low salaries because they constitute a captive source of workers. Many of these people are very well educated and do important work that is essential to the running of the institution.

At one state university, consultants called in to study the pay structure of nonacademic workers divided the administrative staff into two categories: those who work primarily with students and those who work primarily with faculty. They recommended that those who work with faculty have their job descriptions upgraded and thus their salaries raised while those who work with students have their salaries lowered. Most of the workers who benefited were men, while most of the workers—secretaries, school psychologists, career counselors, and financial aid officers—who lost out were women. Can the consultants' presuppositions about the relative value of faculty and students be justified in terms of the goals of an academic institution?

In most schools the responsibility for financial matters is in the hands of the administration. This gives administrators power over the faculty and staff because they decide whether and how many hirings or firings and increases or cutbacks in services are necessary. As a result, faculty and staff often feel that the administrators choose to economize on academic facilities—including faculty positions, faculty salaries, and secretarial and lab positions—while raising administrative salaries, hiring more administrators, and increasing their own power.

In response, the faculty members at some schools have unionized. Unionization is a difficult move for many academics for at least two reasons. First, it formalizes an adversarial relationship between administration and faculty, which is something that academics are reluctant to do. The purpose of the union is to protect its members from mistreatment by the more powerful administration. The ideal of an educational institution—that of a community of scholars dedicated to knowledge—seems to be endangered by the recognition that money, job security, and power are such important issues that unionization is required. Second, unions traditionally argue for salaries and benefits solely on the basis of seniority. This is significantly different from the traditional academic structure, in which salaries and benefits are supposed to be awarded on the basis of academic accomplishment and ability; this change again seems to undermine the purpose of academic work.

Ethical principles encourage us to be kind and friendly toward everyone, to avoid making enemies. But how should we behave when we are in an adversarial relationship that we cannot avoid because it is institutionalized, such as union-management relations? If we anticipate that our adversary will try to exploit us or will not consider our interests, generosity and benevolence are suspended. Trying to maximize benefits for both sides would lessen benefits for the group we have agreed to side with; instead, we try to maximize benefits only for the members of our own group. Does being in a recognized adversarial relationship permit us to treat our adversaries only as means to our own ends, to try to maximize our own benefits even at the expense of the other side? Does the Principle of Universalization help? What about other recognized adversarial situations, such as courts of law? What if everyone belonged to adversarial groups? Would the world be worse, better, or no different?

One problem with academic unions is that they exploit some of the differences in academic ranks. In many places graduate students do a very large proportion of the teaching, but faculty members who have unionized often do not want to accord graduate students equal status in the union. Graduate students are supposed to be temporary employees, apprentices who work in order to learn the craft, receiving very small salaries until they become qualified and move on to permanent jobs.

Unions that exclude research associates, lecturers, graduate teaching assistants, and others who do some of the work of the regular faculty may actually be their own worst enemies. Administrators find that more teaching can be done for less money by graduate students and other part-time teachers who are not protected by the faculty union. Thus, they allot salaries for more nonunion teachers and fewer regular faculty members, thereby undercutting the power of the union by depleting its membership. As organizations to protect individuals with insufficient power from exploitation, unions seem to be morally justified, but it is difficult to justify a union that excludes other powerless individuals (who do some of the same kinds of work) from its protection in order to maximize the power of existing members.

Outside the Institution

Financial support for higher education comes from both public and private sources. The usual justification for using public funds for higher education is that it will benefit everyone, even those who do not directly receive the funds or the results of the education. The community (neighborhood, city, state, or country) needs well-educated scientists, journalists, social workers, medical personnel, and politicians. Some may also say it needs to sponsor and develop the arts, study and preserve its history, and so forth. Certainly many of us are better off because others have had access to advanced knowledge in their fields, but it is not certain that the current system of funding for education is the best one. One continuing problem with applying the Principle of Maximizing Benefits is judging whether current practices do a better job than the alternatives.

Much of the funding for higher education is in the nature of a contract:

student tuition paid in order to learn and get a degree, research contracts for specific work, even fellowship money awarded to faculty members and students to support their studies. Private foundations and government agencies fund nearly all of the most costly research, and this funding enables institutions to support other programs, increase the teaching staff, and so forth. This is possible because granting agencies pay large "overhead" costs to the institution in addition to financing the actual cost of the research.

To the extent that institutions of higher education enter contracts to perform certain tasks with students and with funding agencies, the pursuit of knowledge can be compromised. For example, if half the students in a college suddenly decide to major in computer science rather than English or fine arts, on the contract model the school has an obligation to provide the resources: faculty, courses, and equipment. Without additional funding, this means depriving other programs accordingly. Looked at one way, this indicates that academic worthiness is determined by popularity. Looked at another way, it indicates that academic programs are responsive to the needs and interests of the students and the outside world.

Although it may be commendable to be responsive to student interest, it seems less commendable to allow funding agencies to determine what is taught and researched. For example, when outside funding is available only for the sciences and not the humanities, a balanced liberal arts program is threatened. Specialized programs such as forestry or primate laboratories may be continued by an educational institution only as long as outside funding is available, regardless of the quality of knowledge produced and transmitted by such programs. If the outside funding for these programs lessens, the programs may be dropped, and research in these areas will be abandoned.

Financial support of academic programs often seems like generosity on the part of donors, but there is always a danger that such support can become economic control, determining which research will be done and which subjects will be taught. The danger is increased when the goals of an agency responsible for funding are not educational goals. In the United States considerable support for institutions of higher education comes through the Department of Defense and the military agencies that sponsor research. In recent years institutions of higher education have received nearly $1 billion a year from the Department of Defense for military research (Levey 1983). Much of this research is classified and so is not made available to other scholars or to the public. Some academics object to classified research because secret results are not in the spirit of the academic pursuit of knowledge. Some are also concerned about the morality of accepting money to do research on military weapons systems. One school accepts money to work on parts of a weapon system but refuses to do research on the actual warheads, an indication that the administration feels some qualms about weapons research.

Military agencies also support research that is not directly related to weapons: linguistics, animal behavior, pure mathematics, perception, and many other fields. Some academics argue from the Principle of Maximizing Benefits that it is better to accept money from the Department of Defense than it is not to have the research done at all. One occasionally hears the argument that people opposed to weapons development have a moral duty to divert money from weapons to nonmilitary academic projects.

One may still disapprove of the extent to which the Department of Defense exerts economic control over research that is not directly related to military concerns. Some fear the possibility that if military agencies become the main source of research funding, researchers will become dependent on their support and will be willing to compromise their intellectual goals in order to assure funding. We return to this topic in Chapter 4.

When students and faculty members in colleges and universities disagreed with government policies toward Vietnam, many state legislators voted to reduce funds for higher education. They might have reasoned that with so much political activity going on, with campus strikes and sit-ins, students were not learning as much, and so the education was no longer worth as much money. But many educators, legislators, and taxpayers believed that the reduction in funds was punishment for allowing political activities on campus. In 1983 it became a condition of receiving a student loan that the student register for the draft or have an acceptable excuse. Women students had to give as their "excuse" that they were female in order to receive a loan. Can legislation of this sort be justified? What issues are involved? Do legislators have an obligation not to use public funds to subvert academic freedom or penalize different political views?

The federal government agreed to withdraw its financial support from schools that do not obey nondiscrimination guidelines. When president Ronald Reagan proposed allowing federal funds to be used for Bob Jones' University even though it excluded black students, there were strong public objections, and the proposal was withdrawn. Compare this problem with the one described in the preceding paragraph. Is it morally proper to withhold funds from an institution that practices racial discrimination when the money would improve the quality of education it can provide its students?

People usually think that private individuals may use their own money as they see fit. There does not seem to be anything wrong with private donations to colleges and universities even if they are made on whim for arbitrary or noneducational reasons. Individuals can give money to a school because they are impressed with the beauty of the campus (and the amount of money spent by many private colleges on their buildings and grounds indicates that the look of the campus *is* thought to be an important factor in attracting donations) or because they want to have an effect on the school's development. If someone creates a scholarship for American Indians or endows a chair in paleontology, we think it a generous gift rather than a bribe to influence the direction of the institution. But very wealthy individuals are able to exert significant influence on institutions of higher education by offering money for specified purposes.

It is often possible for an institution to neutralize the controlling effects of conditional endowments. Large donations given for one purpose free money for use in other areas of the institution. But even with these adjustments, the need for private donations creates a danger that institutions will compromise their educational mission in order to maintain financial solvency.

Many institutions of higher education justify expensive intercollegiate athletic programs as investments that bring in more money from fans and alumni. Certainly, athletic success appeals to alumni and other fans, and televised games are more salient and more widely appreciated than research work resulting in Nobel prizes. But critics argue that intercollegiate athletics detract from the educational function of the institution; unless it can be shown how athletic programs are directly important to the educational role of an institution, it is inappropriate to support them even if they raise money for legitimate educational needs. What is the force of this argument? Robert Ludlum (1974) wrote a novel about a college president who organized heroin sales and prostitution to provide money for education. Is legality the only limit to how far an educational institution should go to make money? How about selling used cars?

The policy of one university changed to favor participation in football bowl games, claiming that participation in these athletic activities are very profitable and that although it was not academically worthwhile in itself, it could be used to finance valuable academic programs. Were the athletes being treated only as means? Suppose much of the profit from the bowl games was used to finance the black studies program on the grounds that most of the school's best athletes were black. Should this change our judgment?

It may be argued that athletic training is part of a well-rounded education and deserves as much funding as necessary. However, the Principle of Fairness may require a more equitable distribution of funds among *all* students instead of the special benefits and attention given to the best players on college varsity teams. Is the money spent on the athletic elite like the money spent on equipment for advanced physics courses which also are available only to a small number of students? How much is athletic training like education in other areas? Is there reason to distinguish it from academic areas in which skills are taught, such as language or laboratory courses? Does a comparison of athletic programs with academic subjects indicate that ethical principles should be applied to the two areas in different ways?

RESPONSIBILITIES TO STUDENTS

Most college students lived with their parents before entering college. Some had the full responsibilities of adults, and some were treated like children. If students live at the school, the college has to decide what sort of restrictions and control it is going to exert. An institution of higher education is usually more than a workplace. For many it is a community with social expectations and values that influence the students and other residents. The school must decide whether it is going to try to direct those values, influence them in any way, or ignore them for good or ill.

Even if a school can decide how much to interfere in the lives of its students, this decision may conflict with the views of parents and potential students. Many parents want their children to have continued parental protection; the children usually disagree. If a school exerts too much or too little control, it may find that enrollments decrease. Should a school be more responsive to its students or to their parents, who typically pay for the education? It would be nice if it could be responsive to both, but when there is a conflict, how does it decide where its main obligations lie?

Some schools have many restrictions and exert great control over the lives of their students. Military colleges regulate eating, studying, sleeping, where students can go, and what they wear. Twenty years ago many ordinary colleges had restrictions on dress, required attendance at meals, set curfew hours for women students, maintained sex-segregated dormitories, and in some cases required church attendance. At the same time vandalism, rowdiness, drunk driving, and occasionally shoplifting were serious problems in college communities but were tolerated because the perpetrators were still considered children. Students who broke laws were often saved from criminal prosecution by the college. The college would then decide whether the student's behavior should be punished and how. Although vandalism was often treated lightly, cohabitation or flouting of curfews could be grounds for expulsion. This policy is called *in loco parentis,* because the school acts in the place of parents. Parents have special rights and responsibilities toward their offspring, but it is not clear that college students should be treated as children or that schools have the right or the duty or even the ability to take the place of parents. Whereas parents can deal with each case individually, institutions may be bound by the Principle of Fairness to treat undesirable behavior according to impartial rules. Since the mid-1970s most colleges have imposed fewer restrictions on the personal lives of students. This means that students have more freedom, but it also means that they have less guidance and protection.

Is it fair for a school to save students from criminal prosecution that other citizens are subject to? Is it fair for a school to suspend or expel students whose behavior is not criminal but is considered undesirable? Should schools take parental responsibility for teaching good living habits, transmitting good values to students, or protecting students from bad influences? Should schools encourage students to question the values and principles on which they were raise? Even if one rejects the policy of *in loco parentis,* one may argue that institutions of higher education have a special responsibility to guide the behavior of their students in order to maximize their intellectual development. How sound is this claim?

We often cite individual freedom as a moral value and a reason not to interfere in other people's lives, even when we see that they are making mistakes, acting in the absence of important knowledge, or doing themselves harm. But several ethical principles indicate that we have responsibilities to other people, including the responsibility to interfere for their own good. There may be times when it would be wrong to deny someone knowledge and guidance or even restrictions on freedom that other people have had. For example, we have an obligation to prevent a friend from driving an automobile when drunk. When we consider maximizing benefits, there may be times when the benefits gained might be worth some compromise of individual freedom, for example, in the case of laws regulating prescription drugs. We return to this debate in Chapter 5.

SUMMARY

We first looked at how academic values and moral values may be related and then considered two possibilities: (1) that ethical principles take precedence so that academic practices are worthwhile only when they are morally justified; and (2) that academic values and moral values are independent and may conflict. In particular we considered how the Principle of Fairness is challenged by restricting access to academic resources and by academic institutions that are run as meritocracies rather than democracies. We asked whether knowledge should be considered valuable for its own sake or only as a means to some practical end. This issue is related to the tendency for some academics to hold useful knowledge in low regard. If we accept the claim that academic pursuits need to be justified independently as maximizing benefits, perhaps knowledge should be valued only as a means to practical improvement.

Academic institutions usually try to remain neutral about ethical and political matters in the nonacademic world but cannot ignore the effects of their own policies, such as how their financial investments can support immoral behavior. We considered the ethical role of the academic institution with respect to its community and the larger society, the possibility of exploiting employees, and problems with adversarial union-administration relations. Then we discussed the dangers of accepting significant outside funding from private and governmental agencies that may control the direction of research or even channel it toward immoral purposes. Finally, we discussed the responsibilities a school has toward its students and the conflict between student freedom and the institution's supportive and protective role.

Chapter 3

Hiring and Evaluation of Faculty

This chapter introduces some of the ethical problems involved in an important aspect of the functioning of educational institutions: the hiring and evaluation of academic workers. First we describe the academic hierarchy from chaired professor down through teaching assistant. Next we discuss some institutional considerations that affect hiring and evaluation. We look at the recruiting and hiring of new personnel, at the evaluation of current faculty and at some of the ethical factors involved. Finally, we examine the question of tenure and its relation to academic freedom and the expediencies of modern educational institutions.

THE ACADEMIC HIERARCHY

As in many institutions, the people who work in colleges and universities form a hierarchy. In hierarchical organizations such as the military, where the main dimension is executive control, the chain of command is fairly straightforward from top to bottom. Academic hierarchies are more complex. Our discussion considers only that part of the hierarchy which directly involves the faculty. Because most people outside of academia and many students do not know how colleges and universities are organized, we describe the hierarchy briefly.

Academic institutions try to be meritocracies; that is, benefits and power are distributed to people according to their merits. A meritocracy is not simply a system that gives people what they deserve but a system that determines what sort of things indicate merit. In the academic world merit is supposed to be based on a person's contributions and ability to contribute to knowledge. Reward on the basis of ability or accomplishment seems fair enough, but the picture is more complex. The greatest differences in rewards for the faculty--salary, benefits, and power—occur across academic ranks, and people in different ranks are evaluated in different ways.

In the hierarchy there are three main levels of academic workers. In most institutions there are tenured regular faculty members (usually associate professors and full professors) whose position is practically guaranteed whether they do research or not or whether they teach well or badly, and who are eligible for further merit rewards. There are untenured regular faculty members (assistant professors) with contracts for three to six years who are eligible for tenure if evaluated favorably. Finally, there are irregular (non-tenure-track) faculty members who are not eligible for tenure no matter how long their employment or how good their work; their continued employment is at the discretion of tenured faculty and administrators, usually for one year or one course at a time. Examples of people in this last category include the following:

1. Instructors and "visiting" faculty who are given one- or two-year contracts and may occasionally be considered for promotion to the regular faculty. Some visiting faculty members are on leave from other jobs, but more and more the title is being given to temporary faculty members who have no other job or no place they are visiting from.

2. Lecturers who are usually paid only to teach whether they do research or not and who often have higher teaching loads, no tenure, one-year contracts, and lower salaries.

3. Research associates who are supported by grants to do research and also have short contracts and no tenure.

Often these lesser ranks are filled by people with graduate degrees who are spouses of the regular faculty and form a captive labor pool. Finally, at the bottom of the hierarchy are teaching assistants, usually advanced undergraduates or graduate students who may do anything from grading exams to preparing and teaching several courses. This last group may play a very large role. For example, in one state university they are responsible for fully two-thirds of the classroom instruction. Although these temporary academic employees may do much of the teaching, they are not usually considered part of the academic family but are treated more like hired help.

INSTITUTIONAL CONDITIONS AND SCARCE RESOURCES

During the 1940s and 1950s, in some fields in which it was possible, there were a significant number of scholars who had no regular academic job. Scholarly journals published many articles by authors with no academic affiliation. Many people, including a large proportion of women who are now distinguished in their fields, were employed in temporary positions or not at all. People with independent incomes would work for a nominal dollar a year to gain the institutional affiliation and the benefits of academic life.

But a decade later conditions changed. The number of college students increased enormously, and the financial conditions of colleges improved (partly as a reaction to the Russian Sputnik, the first space satellite). Graduate students about to receive a degree had a relatively easy time finding academic positions. In many fields there were more jobs than candidates with good credentials. Programs and departments expanded rapidly. A well-recommended student from a prestigious graduate program usually had a choice of several good positions; a less fortunate student could almost always find some academic job. Once hired, most faculty members had only to maintain a modest level of competence to be assured of steady advancement up the ranks to full professor. Often there were more or less explicit criteria; even in prestigious institutions, depending on the field, publishing a book or a number of scholarly articles was enough to earn promotion to a tenured rank. In many institutions, just meeting one's classes and sharing in committee work would ensure promotion.

Since the early 1970s the situation has been changing. There are fewer students and much less federal support for higher education. Few academic departments are expanding, and most are cutting back on faculty in number or rank or both. In most academic fields today there are many highly qualified people for every available job. For example, in a recent year there were nine hundred people looking for work in the field of philosophy and only forty tenure-track jobs available in the United States. In most fields an advertised opening for an assistant professor will bring in hundreds of applications. (In contrast, the burgeoning field of computer science and the high salaries offered by industry have attracted many people away from academic jobs and have thus created a scarcity of teachers in this area.)

When resources are scarce, does the current generation of academics have a moral obligation not to benefit at the expense of the next generation of scholars? In the past an abundance of graduate students made academic life much easier for university faculty. For little or no pay, graduate students took on much of the burden of teaching introductory courses, grading exams, leading discussion sections, and doing the donkey work of research, freeing the faculty to teach graduate seminars and do the most interesting parts of research. Furthermore, the need to teach graduate courses served to justify additional faculty positions in each department. This treatment of students could be considered apprenticeship rather than exploitation as long as it was likely that the graduate students would have the opportunity to become professors too. However, this has become a rare opportunity in many fields. Faculty members now have to decide whether self-interest—a light teaching load, time to do research, and other benefits of having an abundance of graduate students—is worth the moral burden of maintaining a large graduate program and recruiting and encouraging new students to serve an apprenticeship when there is little hope of their finding employment as professionals. But is it fair to the graduate students? Are their interests being taken into consideration or are these students being used only as means? Let us look at a specific example.

Although many schools are cutting back their graduate programs, one state university recently instituted a new doctoral program in philosophy. In order to get graduate students for the program, the standards for admission were made lower than at most other graduate programs. The shortage of academic jobs in this field and the poor reputation of this particular department made it nearly impossible for graduates to find teaching positions. Although this university is not promising to place its gradautes in teaching jobs, nearly all students admitted to graduate school in philosophy hope to become professors.

The establishment of this program shows how ethical principles can conflict. On the one hand, the new graduate program can be seen as self-serving because graduate students are recruited to increase the number of courses and supervision hours the faculty can justify to the administration. This makes it more likely that they can expand instead of contracting in the face of diminishing undergraduate enrollment. Additionally, the prestige of the department is increased because it now has a doctoral program. It appears that the new graduate students are only a means for benefiting the faculty, but the department might argue that it is being more democratic than most by allowing nearly anyone the opportunity to get an education in philosophy. Explicit or implicit deception about the benefits of this university's philosophy doctorate can also be considered. Such deception and its effects are discussed in Chapter 5.

Faculty salaries constitute a large part of the budget for a typical college or university. Administrators faced with shrinking economic resources seek ways of getting more teaching for less money. There are two basic ways to do this. One way is to get more teaching out of fewer people, and the other is to reduce the number of faculty members with higher salaries, replacing them with people who can be paid less. Aware of the trade-off between quality and quantity, many schools with shrinking resources try not to increase teaching loads and class sizes beyond a certain point. More commonly administrators try the second course, reducing the relative number of senior people on the faculty. It is not uncommon for a senior full professor to be paid three times what a beginning assistant professor is paid. This means that three new people can be hired for every senior position that is vacated. In addition to the considerable financial advantage, replacing a senior professor with new people also allows a department to add new areas of specialization.

Because of these advantages, some schools are encouraging senior faculty members to retire early by offering financial incentives: continued fringe benefits, partial salaries, or lump-sum awards. Some senior professors even feel a moral obligation to make room for struggling newcomers in the academic community.

It is clear that a school may gain a considerable benefit when a highly paid senior professor retires. Whereas the offering of *positive* incentives to get senior faculty to retire early does not seem to raise any ethical issues, there is a temptation for department heads and college administrators to make things less pleasant for a person they want to get rid of. There have always been ways, both subtle and blatant, to encourage tenured faculty members to leave. Many of the amenities and privileges that faculty members take for granted are under the control of the department head or a higher administrator and are not otherwise part of the faculty contract. An unwanted professor can be appointed to boring or unpleasant committees; be given unpopular teaching schedules with different or less interesting courses every term; be assigned an uncomfortable office or even no office at all; be denied laboratory facilities, research assistants, and teaching assistants; or be given a minimal or no yearly salary increase. These forms of harassment can be very effective. Although the more blatant forms can be redressed by means of a long and costly lawsuit, subtler forms, such as onerous committee assignments and teaching schedules, are nearly impossible to prove.

Department heads and administrators argue that they are trying to maximize benefits when they "encourage" the resignation or retirement of an unwanted senior faculty member. They point to all the good they can do with the salary money released by the vacancy, even though one person may be less well off as a result. Indeed, it may be true that the sum of the benefits derived from the vacancy is greater than the harm done to the senior faculty member *within the context of the immediate situation.* In this weighing, only the benefits and harms of the immediate act are considered. However, consequences *beyond* the particular act of one faculty vacancy can be considered in weighing the harms and benefits. No act can be considered in isolation. Precedents increase the likelihood that similar acts will occur in the future, and so we have to consider the Principle of Universalization. Reactions beyond the immediate situation change the weighing of benefits and harms. For example, it is possible that the forced resignation of one senior professor may seriously affect the morale of other faculty members who fear that they may also become targets for removal for budgetary expediency. In ethical theory such cases are related to "scapegoat" situations in which one person is sacrificed for the greater good of others.

A second way for a school to stretch its budget for faculty salaries is to restrict tenure, promotion, and accompanying salary increases and hire new people at a beginner's salary. In a typical college salary structure three new people can be hired by denying two assistant professors tenure. Although this may seem to be just another harsh financial expediency, deception in recruiting, either deliberate or consequential, may introduce ethical problems. Because schools wish to hire the best candidate available, they try to make their jobs seem attractive. Since job security is an important consideration, schools try to give candidates the impression that they have a good chance of being tenured rather than dismissed after a few years. Some schools have tried to eliminate any deception by designating some or all of their new positions as "terminal" appointments that carry no commitment to consider the jobholder for a permanent position. Some even emphasize that their standard practice is *not* to rehire people at the end of such appointments. However, candidates know that some people *are* rehired at the end of terminal appointments; most people who take such jobs see it as a "foot in the door" and entertain the hope of being one of those who are kept on.

How far must an institution go to prevent people from being harmed because they misjudge the likelihood of their being retained? Does the institution have an obligation to counter unrealistic hopes and estimates of success even though the institution itself never did anything to raise the hopes of the temporary appointee? How is this similar to the university that recruits graduate students for a doctoral program with almost no hope of an academic job afterwards? Many graduate departments mail applicants a statement about the shortage of academic jobs. Consider the analogous problem in business. Does a manufacturer or retailer have an obligation to counter consumers' unrealistic expectations even though the firm is not responsible for engendering them? Are institutions of higher education supposed to act differently?

As financial resources and the number of students have decreased, many untenured faculty members have found that the criteria for promotion have become much more stringent than when they were hired. In some schools where many of the senior faculty members have done little or no research or publishing, junior faculty members are expected to gain national reputations as eminent scholars before they get promoted. Departments are now expected to do more than recommend promotion. They have to defend the qualifications of the junior faculty by writing lengthy and time-consuming briefs to an adversarial administration that tries to minimize the number of promotions. Some departments rarely endorse the junior faculty for tenure because they think they can find someone better (the intellectual grass is greener outside their own institution). Some departments continue to believe this even after years of denying tenure to a long series of replacements—a testimonial to the power of the "grass is greener" myth. Other, less idealistic motivations may be at work. Tenured faculty members may not want to dilute their power by admitting additional members into their ranks. In some schools senior faculty members retain a larger part of the salary budget by limiting the number of people admitted into the higher-paying ranks. There may also be pressure to get rid of junior people whose scholarly and teaching reputations are noticeably superior to those of their senior colleagues. In one department, two assistant professors were fired who each had better credentials than all six of the tenured senior professors combined.

Situations in which faculty members are frequently fired hurt the morale of students whose valued teachers and advisers disappear. They strain the relationship between senior and junior faculty and create a moribund atmosphere in the departments involved. Junior faculty members resent senior faculty members who call for higher standards that the senior members themselves do not meet. Junior faculty members learn to feel little loyalty to the school, to slight their teaching, and to concentrate on academic work that will give them job mobility or use most of their time to train for a new profession. Instead of working for the school, they work for themselves. They find it hard to care about contributing to a school that has no commitment to them and is likely to discard them after their contract is up.

RECRUITING

When academic institutions were better off and when there was less public consciousness about fairness in hiring, most academic jobs were not publicly announced. Instead, job arrangements were made through the "Old Boy Network." Information about openings and candidates was exchanged in letters and telephone calls between friends and professional acquaintances.

The Old Boy Network is often criticized as unfair because it restricts job access to students whose mentors belong to the network. Those who use the network usually do not mean to be immoral but are trying to fulfill obligations by doing the best they can for their friends and students. Before there was awareness that minority groups were being excluded, access to the network was considered a kind of credential, a sign that one had studied with the most influential people in the field. New awareness of systematic inequalities and changes in views about the way the world ought to be have altered our understanding of how to apply the Principle of Fairness. What was once thought to be fair has become unfair, and people who are following certain customs in good faith may find themselves accused of immorality with little warning.

Even if it is unfair, the Old Boy Network is difficult to give up because it makes the arduous recruiting process easier. Publicly advertised academic job openings often produce hundreds of applications. Because there has been an inflation of credentials in academia, many of these applications are supported by recommendations of the highest praise. It is more difficult to evaluate letters of reference from strangers whose main interest is getting *their* students good jobs. Even if one could rely on the honesty of all recommenders, they might not all be good judges of ability, nor would they have as good an understanding of the situation and requirements as someone with close personal knowledge of the recruiting school. Letters from people whom one knows and whose judgment one trusts are taken more seriously than letters from strangers.

Many of the other credentials examined in the recruiting process are gained through Old Boy connections. Schools invite guest lecturers. Most journals invite people to do book reviews and articles and to serve as editorial consultants. Many professional organizations invite people to speak at professional meetings. It takes much more time and effort to publicize the need for a book reviewer or lecturer, wait for applications, and then go through the process of choosing. Each of these invitations becomes a credential on a scholar's curriculum vitae, or academic résumé.

Recently, however, some journals have begun asking for volunteers for book reviews, some professional societies allow any member to present a paper, and some schools have advertised for volunteers for guest lectures (usually because they have no money to pay invited speakers).

In terms of fairness, what is wrong with the Old Boy Network is not that it exists but that some people may have no access to it. This is most serious in academic fields where leading scholars are concentrated in only a few schools. If one has not been educated in those schools and has not been in close contact with the "right" people, one has less opportunity to demonstrate one's ability or disseminate one's work. As we discuss in Chapter 4, intellectual viewpoints that conflict with those held in the elite schools may have little opportunity to be heard. This hampers open discussion and the publication of dissenting views that are essential to the growth of knowledge.

Networks are necessary for academic interactions. When a number of networks exist and new ones can be created, it becomes possible to gain access even if one does not start out from an advantageous position. The public advertisement of job openings is a first step in this direction. Public advertisement is now required by the federal government to comply with antidiscrimination statutes. Whether this requirement actually reduces discrimination is another question, but at least it represents one step toward increasing access to academic contacts and positions.

Although most departments want to hire the best candidate available, criteria for hiring academic workers vary from school to school, from department to department, and even from moment to moment. Many of the criteria cannot be made explicit. For example, applicants are judged on their potential for "collegiality," a quality impossible to define and, to judge by the acrimony in many academic departments, very difficult to predict. Hundreds of applications must be read and sorted in a few days, and the basis for rejection in many cases is an overall impression rather than a checking off of particular features. Because few letters of recommendation give anything but praise, recruiters try to read between the lines. The same words may not strike the same reader the same way at different times. Departments may advertise for one specialty, but by the time candidates are reviewed, the needs are perceived to have changed. All too often one person or faction likes people who do X, and another likes people who do Y. They cannot agree, and so they compromise and look for people who do Z. A mediocre application read after a series of poor ones appears much better by contrast, and the same thing can happen in the other direction. Interviews are not very reliable for predicting long-term ability. The qualities that may help someone do well at an interview—self-assurance and fluency—are less crucial to being a good researcher and teacher. With many applicants and few openings, there are many candidates with approximately the same level of credentials. Within each level, which person is chosen is determined by a complex interaction of so many factors that the process resembles a lottery (Allen 1979).

If this description applied to hiring in business or industry, it might not be so surprising or discouraging. The problem is that academics consider themselves especially well endowed with wisdom, good judgment, and a sense of fairness. We like to pretend that academic hirings are free from bias, whimsy, and prejudice, that people get what they deserve, and that our decisions are *morally* justified.

EQUAL OPPORTUNITY

Laws against discrimination in hiring are fairly recent. For academics who believe that they have always behaved fairly, these laws are a source of irritation and resentment. They require additional paperwork and record keeping and are responsible for the delays and tedium of reading hundreds of applications. Those who believe that academic hiring has been discriminatory find the laws ineffective.

Affirmative action laws say only that if two candidates are "equally" qualified and one is a member of a minority group, the minority person should be hired. However, academic credentials are complex and difficult to compare. It is almost impossible to find any two candidates who are exactly equal in qualifications. One has authored more papers whereas the other has had more teaching experience; one has studied at A and the other at B; one has investigated the subfield of X and the other the subfield of Y. At the crucial final decision in hiring, one or more of these differences in qualifications may appear more important than others and will thus shift the decision toward one candidate over another. Once we decide that one candidate is better than another for whatever reason, it is easy to look at that person's credentials and point to differences in qualifications in order to justify the decision. Since preference for one candidate over another with approximately the same level of credentials is so subjective, it is very easy for unconscious generalizations about the inferiority of one *kind* of person to influence the hiring decision.

This subjectivity in judging qualifications allows academics to ignore affirmative action laws in all but the paperwork. But what about the laws themselves? Because minority group members have been systematically excluded from the academic world in the past, these laws represent attempts to right the balance. If these antidiscrimination laws were obeyed, the number of faculty members who belong to minorities—women, blacks, American Indians, and the like—would slowly increase. Those minority members who were better qualified than white men would no longer be turned down, and those who were equally qualified would also be hired to begin to make up for past exclusion of minorities in academia.

In fact, for two significant minorities these laws have had little effect. The percentage of tenured women actually decreased from 1977 to 1980, while the increase in the percentage of women with full-time academic jobs was negligible (from 25.2 percent to 25.9 percent) considering the increased numbers of women entering the academic job market (Vetter and Babco 1981). Salaries and raises for women faculty members have remained lower than salaries and raises for comparable men. And "the proportion of black faculty members at some of the nation's top universities has remained very small, and in some schools it has actually declined" during the last several years (Butterfield 1984). Affirmative action laws seem to have little effect despite the publicity they have received.

Affirmative action laws have had relatively little effect, but instead of worrying about how to correct social injustice, some academics, particularly in philosophy, have spent much more energy on imaginary situations, arguing that if employers actually favored minorities over white men, it would constitute "reverse discrimination," which would be just as bad as favoring white men over minorites. But this misrepresents the laws, which say only that the minority group member should be chosen if he or she is *equally* qualified. If two candidates are equally qualified, the choice *must* be made on other grounds. Affirmative action laws say that social equality is an overriding reason for breaking the tie in favor of minorities; hiring should not be decided by coin flips or other arbitrary decision methods.

Many philosophers wrote and lectured on the immorality of reverse discrimination. They gave the impression, if only by repetition, that reverse discrimination was a common occurrence instead of a hypothetical problem. Should philosophy and philosophers be held responsible for helping to create this impression? Chapter 5 addresses this problem directly.

Once the question has been raised, we ought to consider—recognizing that this is an abstract question—what ethical principles justify a policy of favoring minority applicants in hiring even if they are apparently *less* qualified than white male candidates. Since favoritism is unfair, it is important to show either that past inequity provides overriding justification or that there is some other moral gain achieved by the policy.

The usual arguments for favoring minorities have been given in terms of reparations to individuals or groups, remedying previous injustices, and the like. But perhaps the strongest argument is that membership in a minority group is *itself* a qualification. Minority faculty members provide role models for minority students and richer learning experiences for nonminority students. Because minority group members have experiences that differ from those of the dominant culture, they increase the variety of perspectives available and can provide a critical scrutiny of claims that might remain unquestioned in a more uniform group. It seems reasonable that sharing minority membership might help establish rapport between faculty and students and that a minority faculty member could serve as a concrete example that other members of that group will have opportunities in academia.

Is there any evidence that it is important for students to have role models? One interesting statistic is that more girls than boys complete every grade through high school. As the percentage of male teachers increases through the grades, so also does the percentage of boys completing that grade. At the college level, where there are more male teachers, particularly in the positions of highest authority, more men than women complete their studies each year. This correlation certainly suggests that the decrease in role models for women affects their schooling. It also suggests that the presence of fewer role models for boys in early grades affects their success. However, the existence of role models is probably not the only factor affecting these statistics.

EVALUATION

Some rewards in the academic world do not depend directly on how one is evaluated: the excitement of research and the joys of discovery, inspiring students and colleagues, doing one's job well and having interesting work. Not every academic gains these rewards; for some, working conditions are poor, students are apathetic, and colleagues are dull. But many other rewards, including the most tangible, all depend on the results of evaluation: academic honors such as fellowships; grants; invitations to lecture, attend, or moderate conferences; appointment to professional offices inside and outside one's institution; honorary societies; and chaired professorships as well as pay raises, promotions, and job security in the form of tenure. There are also less formal rewards that come from positive evaluations: respect from students and admiration and acceptance from colleagues.

There is a danger that any evaluation can be mistaken or unjust. The ethical problems involved are not unique to institutions of higher education. (What may be unique to academia is a self-righteousness about the evaluations, a belief that decisions can be kept free of prejudice and personal whim. This comes about because academics, by the nature of their profession, see themselves as experts in clear reasoning and balanced, rational judgment.) The ethical issues special to academic evaluations are raised by the criteria used, the decisions about who can contribute to the evaluation, and the role of the tenure system in evaluative judgments.

What Is Evaluated

Most evaluations of academic workers consider three areas: research, teaching, and service to the institution. An institution committed to the pursuit of knowledge has to decide how much to emphasize teaching (conveying existing knowledge) and how much to emphasize research (finding new knowledge). Because a faculty member has limited time and energy, and because the audiences and the activities for teaching are usually different from those for research, these activities are often in competition. Faculty members find themselves interrupting research to prepare classes or neglecting class preparation in order to work on research. There are times when research and teaching complement each other, but often the demands of one are in conflict with the demands of the other.

In many academic institutions research is valued more than teaching. With few exceptions teaching is the one job that faculty members must do to collect a salary, but often they are evaluated and rewarded primarily on the basis of research. This is true even of many colleges that think of themselves primarily as teaching institutions. The people whose main function is teaching (for example, lecturers and teaching assistants) usually have lower status.

There are several reasons for this. First in an academic institution, those with the most knowledge are likely to be the most valued and respected. Students are likely to have the least knowledge and faculty members the most. Therefore, work done at the institution that is addressed to students is likely to be less respected than work addressed to other faculty members. Except for differences in level, teaching and research may actually involve similar activities: setting up laboratories and experiments, interpreting texts, explaining research through lectures and writing, and answering questions. But research is still valued more than teaching because it is addressed to a higher-status audience.

Second, contributing new knowledge is likely to be valued more than organizing and transmitting old knowledge. This occurs not because new knowledge is intrinsically worth more than old knowledge. Older knowledge has stood the test of time and is likely to be more valuable than new research results, many of which are trivial or will be revised or discarded later. Rather, it is because our culture values newness, originality, and creativity far more than oldness, loyalty to tradition, or faithful preservation. Again, we can ask how these values are related to academic values and ethical values.

Students, with some faculty support, have argued that teaching should be considered more important to evaluations of the faculty. One argument compares students to consumers and invokes concepts of justice and contractual obligation. Students and their families who pay tuition and taxes for education should get good value in return, and students get more value from the direct benefit of good teaching than from the indirect benefits of good research. Although faculty members may value research more than teaching because it addresses questions of interest to themselves, students are their clients, with the *right* to primary consideration. Even for those who consider research contributions of primary importance, one can argue that an outstanding teacher is more likely to increase the number of talented researchers in the next generation of scholars. Thus, the devaluing of teaching is actually shortsighted because it reduces the pool of future research talent.

One response to this argument is that knowledge has to be nurtured, protected, and studied by experts for the students' benefit and protection. False information and misleading theories can do as much harm as poisonous consumer products. We need experts to test what is taught just as we need agencies and licensing bureaus to protect us from dangerous products. Tuition and tax monies for education are not just for teaching but also for research, that is, to study what will be taught. It is shortsighted to look only at the end product—the teaching—and suppose that this is all that is necessary for good education.

The argument is often made that people who do no research are not able to teach well because they are less likely to know about and be able to evaluate the new developments in their fields. Thus they are more likely to transmit false or out-of-date information. This argument has merit, but many universities that stress research use people with little or no research experience to do a very large proportion of the teaching. This practice undercuts the force of the argument, making it seem hypocritical.

A fair and thorough evaluation of a faculty member's research is a difficult task, but it is even harder to evaluate the quality of an instructor's teaching. Faculty members rarely attend the classes of their colleagues, and when they do they are likely to observe atypical events, either showcase lectures or nervous performances by junior colleagues who know their careers may depend on how well they perform. Faculty members sometimes hear about a colleague's teaching from students, but usually the number of reports is too small to be reliable. Furthermore, because of the asymmetry of power and the difficulty of soliciting opinions without giving any hint of one's own biases, there is a danger that students are likely to tell senior professors what they want to hear.

Many colleges have begun to use information from evaluation forms filled out anonymously by students. If a large proportion of students actually submit these forms, they can be a useful source of information about teaching skill. However, many faculty members believe that students are not the best judges of good teaching. They believe, for example, that students do not have the background to know whether a teacher is presenting only the "juicy" aspects of a field or presenting a complete picture. The ethical danger of using student ratings is that teachers whose professional lives are at stake will direct their efforts toward gaining high evaluations from students instead of trying to do the most effective teaching. When teacher evaluation forms appeared on their campuses, some assistant professors report that they changed their behavior in ways they thought would improve their ratings, regardless of whether they thought it would improve their teaching. In particular, they avoided giving failing grades and gave out more A grades, made their exams easier, avoided challenges that might be frustrating, made efforts to appear friendly and accessible to students without actually investing more time, and tried to use movies and entertaining demonstrations in class. What they were doing was trying to improve their reading on the instrument that measures teaching quality rather than improving their teaching quality directly. To the extent that the instrument can be manipulated independently of the behavior it is intended to measure, teaching quality can actually worsen. It is ironic that the introduction of teacher evaluation forms, which are supposed to improve teaching quality, may in some cases have the opposite effect.

The ethical problem here is whether students should have a voice in deciding who their teachers are to be. The issue is related to the ethical justification for laws that protect people from harming themselves: building codes, prescription drug laws, and aircraft seat belt regulations, for example. In each of these realms citizens are not permitted to decide for themselves what they will do; laws based on expert opinion preempt control. Such laws seem reasonable when it is clear that the average citizen is not in a position to make an informed judgment about the product or activity involved. Although it is probably true that faculty members, as experts in their fields, would be better than students at judging the quality of a colleague's teaching *given the same information*, it is extremely rare, as we have discussed, that they *do* have the same information. Therefore, student evaluations of teachers are still likely to be better than faculty assessments. In Chapter 5 we discuss further the weighing of student and faculty judgments.

Unusually strong student evaluations of teachers may be minimized or discounted by envious faculty members who suspect that a more appreciated colleague is pandering to student tastes (Van den Berghe 1970), and negative student evaluations may be culled to use as evidence against an unpopular colleague. But student evaluations of *teaching* are given at least token consideration in many hiring and evaluation decisions. In contrast, students, even graduate students, are not consulted on evaluations of faculty research, although many of them have strong opinions. To allow students to evaluate faculty research as well as teaching goes against the order of hierarchical organization of educational institutions. Perhaps it is the preservation of this hierarchical structure that helps keep student evaluations, and hence consideration of teaching, in a minor role.

THE TENURE SYSTEM

It may be misleading to talk of evaluations as if they were uniform throughout academic life when tenure evaluations for most academics eclipse all others. Before tenure, an employee is on probation. One may be an excellent teacher and researcher and a devoted employee, but if one's department thinks it can do better or if economic, political, and other factors intervene, one may be evaluated negatively and fired. After being granted tenure, faculty members have virtually guaranteed employment. One may be a poor teacher, a poor researcher or nonresearcher, or an uncooperative employee, but even if one's department knows it can do better, one cannot usually be dismissed from one's position. As mentioned earlier, even tenured faculty members can be made miserable enough that they will want to leave. Theoretically, even tenured faculty members *can* be fired, but unlike the situation that exists before tenure, the burden of proof has changed. Instead of a department having to show that someone is the best available in order to keep that person employed, it now has to show that the person is completely incompetent, unable to conduct classes, or guilty of moral turpitude in order to fire that person.

The main defense of tenure is that it protects academic freedom—the freedom of a faculty member to do research and teach in areas that may be unpopular with colleagues or administrators. However, tenure protection can be abused. At many institutions a tenured professor who does no research and does the barest minimum of teaching and committee work can collect a full year's salary for about two hundred hours of work. Some have argued that abusers of the tenure system drain the financial resources of the institution and also tie up positions that could be filled by people who would contribute much more to the pursuit of knowledge.

Tenure guarantees professors only the right to their positions; it does not commit the institution to maintaining those positions. It is possible to fire unwanted tenured faculty members who cannot be cajoled or coerced into quitting. If the school eliminates the position entirely—for example, eliminates its entire philosophy department as Rockefeller University did—tenure is no protection. Anyone in that position is fired. One state university was unhappy with its Portuguese department. The department had grown because it encouraged student athletes to take its courses by grading leniently. When the foreign language requirement was abolished, athletes stopped taking the courses, and the department's enrollment diminished dramatically. But members of the department had tenure, and so the university eliminated the entire department. It fired all the tenured faculty of that department and then rehired a few into an enlarged Spanish department. Another school closed down entirely, firing its entire faculty. It reopened the next day under a new name and rehired only those faculty members it wanted to keep, claiming that this move was necessary to trim away the academic "deadwood" (Winkler 1983).

Although such dodges violate the spirit of tenure, defenders argue that the actions are justified. They claim that "working to rule," or doing the legal minimum of work, is a violation of the spirit of tenure protection, which is designed to protect controversial intellectual contributions, not absence of contribution. Therefore, the spirit of the tenure agreement has already been broken by the other party. Inactive faculty members are not doing their fair proportion of the intellectual work of the school, and so it is unfair to keep them on. They further argue that while firing unproductive faculty members causes harm to those who are fired, this is outweighed by the benefit to colleagues, students, and the larger community gained by replacing them with intellectually active scholars. Thus, the benefits are maximized.

Those who criticize the circumvention of tenure protection compare tenure to the legal principle of the presumption of innocence. It does happen that some guilty people beat the system and escape punishment, they argue, but it is far more important to avoid making a mistake by punishing the innocent. The analogy for the tenure system is that some deadwood is the cost of preserving academic freedom and preventing the dismissal of someone whose ideas the people in power do not like. Suspending an important principle when someone judges that it is being abused can set a dangerous precedent. What constitutes an abuse? Suppose an administrator or another faculty member decides that some kinds of research do not constitute "legitimate" intellectual contributions? This introduces just the sort of violation of academic freedom that tenure is supposed to prevent. We return to this argument in Chapter 4.

These arguments defend the existence of tenure but not the withholding of it from the junior faculty. Perhaps they, more than anyone, need the academic freedom it provides. Theoretically, tenure is granted after six years of work (occasionally less), after scholars have had a chance to prove themselves. However, with shrinking budgets, fewer positions, and a surplus of scholars, colleges and universities are looking for national reputations based on large numbers of publications that take more time to produce. Therefore, the actual time without tenure can be ten years or more. This lengthening of the probationary period means that a growing proportion of scholars must exist without tenure protection for a longer and longer period, until they have national reputations and many publications. The system also pressures scholars to avoid bold and untried directions in their research. Scholars whose research is unpopular (at least with those judging them for tenure) or who are critical of the research of their senior colleagues are less likely to get tenure. Thus, the very people who most need the protection of academic freedom provided by tenure (the controversial scholars) are the least likely to receive it. Withholding tenure until the end of a probationary period is a compromise. Because some faculty members will not be productive scholars, the untenured period provides a chance to discover who they are before bestowing the strong protection of tenure for their academic freedom. But during this time scholarly productivity is artificially stimulated by the threat of tenure decisions and artificially constrained by the lack of academic freedom.

It seems impossible to conceive of a modern institution of higher education without some hierarchical structure. But there is a danger that the strictly delineated system of academic ranks fosters more respect for privilege and power than for wisdom and innovation.

Are there other ways of protecting academic freedom that would be more equitable than withholding tenure from junior faculty? Some colleges, Hampshire College and Bennington College for example, have no tenure system. Instead they conduct periodic reviews of the faculty. What are the advantages and disadvantages of this system? What about junior faculty members who do innovative or controversial research? Are they in danger of never having a tenured job? Is it better to have colleagues who are all in the same situation? Should all faculty members be required to do a certain amount of research or teach a certain number of students in order to retain tenure? Can a comparison with some other protective system (unions or families) that is subject to abuse help in the analysis?

SUMMARY

Evaluating the quality of ideas and of those who produce and transmit them is central to academia. Institutions of higher education are modeled on meritocracies (systems that reward according to merit as defined by academic ability or accomplishment) rather than democracies. The hierarchical structure of academic institutions and the different levels of power introduce potential conflicts between the academic values of meritocracy and the ethical principles of Fairness and of Maximizing Benefits. Increasing competition for academic jobs has increased power differences and the potential for exploitation of junior workers, including graduate students. We looked at the recruiting process, the goal of equal opportunity, affirmative action laws, and the difficulties of applying the Principle of Fairness. Next we looked at the evaluation process itself, at what counts as a credential and who does the evaluating. Then we discussed the tenure system, the goal of protecting academic freedom, the restriction of that protection to the senior faculty, and the problems of such a system.

Chapter 4

Ethical Problems in Research

Ethical problems arising from the research conducted in institutions of higher education can be divided into five topic areas:

1. Consequences of research and how the findings affect the institution, the society at large, and the ecology.
2. Research subjects, both human and animal, and their rights to informed consent, privacy, and minimal suffering; justifications for deception, risk, and pain in research.
3. Priorities in research: topic choice, quality versus quantity, and the influence of the academic reward system.
4. Cheating in research: data dubbing and falsification, misrepresentation of results, the means versus ends problem in scholarly cheating.
5. Stealing ideas and credit, priority of discovery and publication, patronage and assigning credit for authorship, plagiarism from the work of colleagues and students.

CONSEQUENCES OF RESEARCH

The consequences of scholarly research have raised ethical problems as far back as the time of Socrates, who was sentenced to death because his inquiries were claimed to have threatened social stability. Contemporary examples include the decisions of scientists working on the Manhattan Project to develop the atomic bomb, objections to the study of human behavior in order to control and change it, and concern about the dangers of biological catastrophe resulting from an unforeseen consequence of gene-splicing research.

Skinner (1972) argues that we need to study behavior in order to control it, for example, to manipulate social conditions so that wars can be prevented and more students will enjoy school. Some people counter that Skinner's goal is misguided and unattainable, but others argue that it is immoral. Is it immoral to look for ways to change the environment so that people will want to learn more, obey the law, and avoid war? How about getting people to work harder, be religious, and get and stay married? What about getting people to obey authority? Is all research aimed at controlling people immoral or does it depend on what we want them to do?

Most of the researchers who joined the Manhattan Project weighed their participation in the development of a weapon that would cause unprecedented death and destruction against the likelihood that such a weapon would be developed and used by Nazi Germany. On the surface, the research in recombinant DNA also involves a straightforward although difficult dilemma: The risks have to be weighed against the anticipated benefits of the biological product under development. But many cases are far from clear. For example, we do not yet know the potential benefits of the production of human interferon and other organic molecules by genetically altered microorganisms. Speculation has ranged from the modest claim that it will reduce the severity of the common cold to claims that it will wipe out cancer. On the other hand, some people worry that a plague organism may be created. How can we decide whether the potential benefits of the research are worth the potential dangers? The nature and likelihood of the risks may be very hard to evaluate. For example, some scientists thought that there was a small but real chance that the first nuclear explosion would spread beyond the lump of uranium in the bomb itself and destroy instantly the atmosphere or even the entire planet. What should they have done? How does one decide?

Since research is the study of what is not yet known, the potential benefits and risks can be especially difficult to evaluate. In areas where dangers are well known—work with radioactive substances or rocket launches, for example—the research project must be approved by a federal regulatory agency or an institutional review board (IRB) within the school. However, neither the researchers nor the review boards are going to be completely impartial. Those who are expert enough to judge the safety of research projects are likely to be acquainted with the researchers, accept the research methods ordinarily employed, and consider the research more interesting and beneficial than disinterested outsiders would. It is difficult to know who should get to decide about research that may affect everyone when only a few are knowledgeable enough to assess the consequences. The problem is even more serious when the experts are affected by the consequences differently from the rest of the population.

For example, consider the evaluation of the risks and benefits of a program to create a cancer vaccine by mutating viruses. The research would require many years and a commitment of millions of dollars of public funds. The risks include not only the possibility that large amounts of money, time, and human resources may be wasted on a failure but also the possibility that the research itself will accidentally produce a very dangerous virus. If the researchers succeed, they as individuals are likely to benefit enormously in terms of immense personal satisfaction, scientific and popular recognition and fame, and perhaps even wealth. Even if they do not succeed, they will have several years of interesting work at good salaries and a chance to continue cancer research on another project later. If the vaccine is found and becomes universally available, the researchers, along with everyone else, will be free from the threat of getting cancer. The cost-benefit analysis for the members of the research team is very different from that for the members of the population at large. The researchers share the same possible benefits and risks of disease as everyone else, but they receive additional benefits: the use of public funds, satisfying and important work, and a chance at fame and success. It would be hard for them to evaluate the worth of their project in the same way that others might. This issue shows that it is hard to apply the Principle of Maximizing Benefits where potential harms and benefits are not shared equally by everyone who is affected.

Not only might some research project destroy a planet or start a plague, indirect harm may be done through knowledge of the research results; that is, people may misunderstand the results or panic at the knowledge. When evaluating research proposals involving risk, one can argue that *suspecting* that something significant may be true and not doing the research to find out would set a dangerous precedent. Universalizing such an action is dangerous. If one refrained from research because it *might* have negative consequences, one would have to give up a large proportion of research projects. The consequences of having a general rule to refrain from dangerous research could be very harmful if too much research was curtailed. The consequences of having a general rule to allow and protect all research would probably be beneficial in the long run, with the benefits outweighing the harmful consequences of the few exceptional cases. Still, each project has to be judged individually. Setting a precedent is one of the factors that has to be considered: *Will* preventing a particular project license or encourage the prevention of other worthwhile projects?

Suppose a research team investigates the possibility that a significant portion of a racial or ethnic group is genetically more prone to violent loss of temper. What will a positive finding mean for the way in which society treats this group? Will insurance companies require the more emotionally unstable group to pay higher rates on liability insurance? Will members of this group find it harder to be hired as airline pilots or police officers, jobs where loss of temper is a serious liability? Will public school teachers have an automatic expectation that children belonging to this group are the likely instigators of schoolyard fights? Public knowledge of such a result could be a serious handicap for members of the group. Should the research be conducted at all if such a handicap for a racial or ethnic group is likely to result?

There could be benefits to such a finding. Perhaps people should know that they have to be especially careful not to provoke a member of the group, just as we all take special care not to provoke a person we know to be in a bad mood. One might claim that social relations in general would be improved by such research. On the other hand, the research may create a social liability for these people: a pariah status imposed on group members. Or if the group is large and powerful enough, the research may provide a license for its members to behave violently, condoning such behavior because it is "natural." How likely are these consequences? How would they depend on the strength of the tendency and the social standing of the group? Suppose the research showed that the tendency toward loss of temper occurred in 45 percent of people with Irish and American Indian ancestors? Twenty-five percent of blue-eyed males?

One way to justify such a research project would be to show that the benefits of discovering such a difference would be greater than any harm that would be caused. But would this be enough? Should the benefits and harm to the group concerned be weighed more heavily than those to the population at large? Is there a danger of treating members of this group as objects only, mere means to social order, and not as ends in themselves?

In the 1960s some people claimed that their research findings showed that blacks were genetically inferior to whites in intelligence. There was a great furor about this research, with many arguing that it should never have been done. Amid this furor, articles showing that the research methodology of these projects was seriously flawed and that the conclusions were unjustified went practically unnoticed (see Scarr-Salapatek 1971). Although academics of all disciplines were willing to discuss the morality of the IQ research, with many assuming it to be correct, only a few were able to evaluate the way the research was done. Is there a special danger that research claims will be accepted without question by a public that is not in a position to evaluate the research?

There is always a possibility that someone may adapt research results that were intended for the good of humanity to evil purposes. Therefore, we cannot expect the researchers themselves to be responsible for *all* the consequences of their work, just as we are not held responsible if our good deeds are somehow twisted by others. But this does not allow researchers to ignore entirely the consequences of their work. Tom Lehrer (1981) wrote a song about a missile scientist who declines reponsibility for the consequences of his research:

> "Once the rockets are up, who cares where they come down?
> That's not my department," says Wernher von Braun.

Research does not originate from a value-neutral position. The questions asked and the problems studied are the ones considered interesting, worthwhile, and important. The criteria that determine what is interesting, worthwhile, and important are often based on ethical values.

Suppose you are offered a job studying whether porpoises with magnetic cylinders strapped to their backs can be trained to swim up to ships. Can you evaluate the morality of this project in isolation, or is it your responsibility to consider how the results of your research might be used? How far must you consider? Can you think of apparently innocent or beneficial research projects that could be turned to immoral ends? Can you think of any research project that is *impossible* to turn to immoral ends?

Many psychological theories of personality development and political theories of the nature of government assume that people are basically interested only in themselves and are only derivatively interested in the well-being of other people (Wallach and Wallach 1983). Yet many people are very interested in the well-being of some other people, and some people are more interested in the well-being of others than in their own. Do such theories actually encourage unethical behavior by depicting selfish behavior as normal?

RESEARCH SUBJECTS

When a geologist cuts into a geode or a ceramic engineer pressures a sample to the breakdown point, the performance of the experiment is unlikely to raise any ethical issues. But this may not be true in other fields, especially the biological and social sciences. The investigations of a physiologist cutting into the brain of a living animal or a psychologist pressuring a subject to the breakdown point do raise ethical issues. These issues have been squarely confronted, and a number of principles have been formulated to guide research that is done on living creatures (American Psychological Association 1972 and 1973). Federal granting agencies and professional organizations have guidelines that incorporate these principles. The first two guidelines are based on the Principle of Not Treating People Only as Means. The last two are based on the Principle of Maximizing Benefits. Here they are in brief.

1. Humans must be freely willing to serve as experimental subjects; they cannot be forced or coerced. This is the Principle of Voluntary Participation.
2. Human subjects should have enough information to make an informed choice about whether to participate. This is the Principle of Informed Consent.
3. Subjects should not have to experience unnecessary stress, pain, and (for humans) loss of privacy, nor should they be exposed to unnecessary risks of lasting physical or psychological damage.
4. The benefits of the knowledge gained from the research should be worth the investment in time, effort, energy, and risk undertaken by the subjects.

The first principle forbids any research, no matter how great its anticipated value, in which human subjects are forced against their will to participate. Whether they are hospital patients, prisoners, college students, or people at shopping malls, all must agree to take part in any experiment. They must not be forced, coerced, or threatened.

But there are ways of inducing cooperation or persuading people to participate that are more subtle than physical force or outright threat. Participating in an experiment may be less repugnant than the alternatives one is given. People who are dying often choose to undergo an experimental medical procedure even though it offers them only a small chance of being saved. People who need money desperately are very likely to agree to be experimental subjects if they are well paid. Prisoners are likely to agree to participate in experiments in order to increase their chances for parole. College students sign up for experiments to fulfill course requirements or to please their instructors. Shoppers will fill out questionnaires and try products for money, free samples, or a chance to be on television. Inducements in the form of hope, money, or credit are routinely offered to experimental subjects. When these inducements are not overwhelming and when the alternatives are not terrible, we can say that participation was freely chosen. But when the alternatives are seen as terrible—certain death, starvation, imprisonment, or even a low grade or a professional setback—it is not so clear that the choice is free.

In addition, the way the alternatives are presented to potential subjects may have a lot to do with whether they choose to participate. The Principle of Voluntary Participation is meaningless without knowing what one is volunteering for. The Principle of Informed Consent requires that potential subjects understand what procedure awaits them; what the experience will cost them in terms of time, effort, stress, pain, and loss of privacy; and what risks there are of lasting physical or psychological damage.

However, just as it is difficult to anticipate what the general consequences of research are, it may be difficult to assess the consequences for a particular subject. The experience may be easy for some people and stressful for others; there may be side effects for some and not for others. Subjects may not really understand what will happen to them, or they may not be able to appreciate the actual costs and risks. For example, a person warned that a dental procedure "may be a bit painful" often has a different feeling about the procedure when in the middle of it.

When risk to the subject is involved, there is a further problem with the Principle of Informed Consent. To the extent that potential subjects are unable to appreciate the *magnitude* of risk in an experiment, they are not capable of giving their informed consent to participate. Yet except for those with formal training in probability, people do not correctly appreciate the magnitude of risks, especially when small probabilities of bad outcomes are involved (Cohen 1960 and 1964). People mistakenly think that events with good consequences (for example, winning a lottery) are more likely than they really are and that events with bad consequences (for example, being in an automobile accident) are less likely.

People's choices are influenced not only by what they are told but by *who* tells them. Most patients routinely accept the advice of their doctors, even when they are advised to undergo experimental treatment. Experts who are best able to give advice about participating in an experimental procedure are frequently experimenters themselves and thus may have some interest in seeing the experiment done. Experimenters may be in positions of power or may be connected to those with power over potential subjects so that their recommendations, however obviously self-interested, carry a force that other self-serving advice would not. For example, nonpaying medical clinic patients may believe (sometimes correctly) that participating in an experiment is required in order to receive any treatment.

Imagine a situation where a graduate student's thesis supervisor asks the student, "If you have a few minutes to spare, would you mind helping me out by being a subject in an experiment I'm running?" How likely is the student to decline? If the same request were made by a fellow student, would there be the same pressure to accede?

Birth control pills were tested on Puerto Rican women several years before they were allowed on the market in the continental United States. Thus, women in the continental United States were deprived of an effective method of birth control for several years. At the same time this may be seen as exploitation of minority women, particularly if dangerous side effects are greater than the benefits. How does this compare with the testing of the Salk polio vaccine, where in order to test its rate of effectiveness, half the children were given saltwater placebo while the other half received the vaccine. (The children given the placebo were later given the vaccine, but only after enough time went by so that a statistically significant number of them got polio.) Do arguments about maximizing benefits work here? How does the problem of distributing the benefits enter? Can such arguments lead to unwanted conclusions when a few experimental subjects unfairly have to bear too large a risk? Are such subjects being treated as means only?

Occasionally the Principle of Informed Consent is deliberately compromised because the value of the research is considered to outweigh the partial loss of the subject's rights. In certain kinds of experiments, usually in psychology and pharmacology, subjects are either deliberately misinformed or kept ignorant about at least some aspects of the procedure or purpose of the experiment. This is done, for example, in order to study the reactions of people under conditions when they are not expecting what will happen to them or when they would behave differently if they knew what was going on.

One famous experiment was conducted by Milgram (1963) in which the subjects believed they were helping to develop important new methods of teaching. The subject served as a teacher helping a learner (who was really the experimenter's accomplice) memorize a list of words by administering an electric shock after each mistake. The experimenter directed the subject to increase the shock level each time the learner made a mistake. The actual purpose of the experiment was to see how far people would follow the orders of the experimenter to deliver stronger and stronger electric shocks despite the protests and cries of the learner. The very nature of the study required that the subject be ignorant of its purpose. Subjects found the role very stressful whether they were in the majority who refused to complete the experiment or the minority who did go all the way. Milgram tried to minimize the harm done to subjects by providing psychological counseling after the experiment.

Subjects in this experiment were like secret agents who accept an assignment without knowing its true purpose. It was a very stressful experience for many of the people who participated. But it was Milgram who made the judgment that the stress experienced by the subjects was a worthwhile trade-off for knowledge about the limits of obedience to authority.

Although Milgram's experiment would no longer be approved by a review board, it illustrates a method currently used in many psychology and pharmacology experiments. The Principle of Informed Consent is applied in a modified fashion: Subjects are told in general terms what the experimental experience will be like before they participate, but the actual purpose and details of the experiment are diguised. However, the modified Principle of Informed Consent requires that there be nothing in the actual experiment that subjects would object to if they were told about it beforehand. In such cases the cost to the subject and the value of the research— Principles 3 and 4—must be considered more carefully.

For example, potential subjects may be told that the experiment requires them to watch a movie on automobile accidents. A person who wants to avoid this experience may then refuse to participate. However, the experimenter is caught between the requirement to warn the subject about what the experience of viewing the film will really be like and making the experimental manipulation as effective as possible (such films are used for shock value to create high emotional levels). The less warning the subject has, the more effective the manipulation (Hunt 1982).

Experiments involving deception have also been criticized because they sanction using unethical means to gain beneficial ends, in other words, deception for the sake of knowledge. Critics argue that using deception in a respected context such as scholarly research gives status to unethical behavior, making it more likely that deception will appear in other contexts. This will result in a general lowering of mutual trust and will cause serious harm to human society. This pessimistic prediction actually did come true in miniature. During the 1960s one university psychology department conducted many experiments involving deception. Knowledge of this practice soon spread among the undergraduates who were used as experimental subjects. As a result, the subjects became enormously skeptical, trying to out-guess the experimenter. Ths subjects were so distracted from the experimental tasks that the results suffered noticeably. Some subjects even admitted that they tried to pay back the experimenter's deceit by producing spurious or contrary data.

When experimental subjects are members of another species, they are not told the purpose of the research, and their consent is never required. Animal subjects of experimental procedures are either captured or bred to serve this purpose. Federal regulations are now strict about the *living* conditions of experimental animals, setting standards for ventilation, cleanliness, and so on. (In one case, the animal cages at a university research facility were moved to graduate student offices and the graduate students were moved to the animal rooms so that conditions for the animals met federal standards. There are no such standards for graduate students.) However, it is much more difficult to specify general rules about the *experimental* conditions for the animals. Review boards consider whether experiments will cause the animals *unnecessary* pain, but *painless* operations that remove large portions of an animal's brain or result in death are not prohibited (Singer 1975; Adams 1978).

Suppose you are on an experimental review board. You receive a proposal that dogs be given enormous electric shocks in situations where they are helpless to prevent them. The stated purpose of the experiment is to see how dogs, and perhaps people, behave when they are helpless to prevent awful events. The experimenters suggest that this experiment will tell us something about the plight of cancer patients, concentration camp victims, and perhaps also people in the most downtrodden sectors of society. Should this experiment be approved? Why or why not? What conflicting values does the answer depend on?

Suppose an institutional review board receives a proposal to remove a portion of the brain of rats in order to study the possibility that that portion suppresses extrasensory perception (ESP) waves. This operation causes the rats to die after the experiment is over, but the discovery of a way to stimulate ESP waves would be an impressive find. Should the committee approve the experiment? Would it make a difference if chimpanzees were the subjects? How is the judgment about the value of ESP research, the plausibility of the particular project, and the phylogenetic level of the subjects related to the judgment about whether it is ethically acceptable? Is the use of animal subjects for experimental purposes an example of treating others only as means rather than as ends in themselves?

Institutional review boards are recent additions to the academic world, representing a clear recognition that academic pursuits are subject to ethical constraints. But there are other constraints on research, some of which may conflict with ethical principles.

PRIORITIES IN RESEARCH

Unless ethical principles are violated, academic freedom, which entails the freedom to do research in any area, is highly valued by academics and is explicitly or implicitly protected by the charters or bylaws of many institutions of higher education. Academic freedom implies protection from financial, political, and religious constraints. Galileo and La Mettrie were persecuted for discovery and intellectual heresy. We know of their work today because they managed to escape persecution and keep their ideas alive. However, many lesser-known scholars were punished for doing unpopular research or were denied academic resources. We do not know how many great discoveries and ideas were so effectively suppressed that we never learned of them.

Academic freedom can be justified on ethical grounds. It can be considered a basic freedom, like freedom of speech. Or one can argue that the consequences justify it, that the growth of knowledge is critical to the development of civilization and thus benefits the species. This source of benefits should be protected against any kind of constraint. There may be powerful influences that want to encourage or suppress research done on military weapons, proofs of the existence of God, or the relation of sexual decadence to the downfall of Rome. But in order to find truth we need a haven where scholars can study topics that may be unpopular, controversial, or without practical benefit. The principle of academic freedom requires that we protect unpopular research and research that may even seem immoral to many people. Unpopular truths are truths nonetheless. If God does not exist, if sexual promiscuity increases longevity, if mental ability is related genetically to some ethnic, sexual, or racial groups, it can be argued that we should know these things.

Or should we? Earlier in this chapter we considered whether it is always morally good for a truth to be known and whether there may be some truths that can cause more harm than good. However, the reasons for protecting academic freedom are similar to the reasons for protecting freedom of the press. Although there may be particular cases where uncovering and publishing the truth will do more harm than good, in general it would be much worse to limit these activities. What seems especially dangerous is the possibility that a few people hold the power to decide what knowledge is to be sought.

Although academic freedom is nearly always protected from outside interference and pressures, institutions of higher education are not as worried as they should be about inside interference and pressures. It is not unusual, and it is even expected in many places, for senior faculty members to have a strong influence on what research projects are selected by the junior untenured faculty. This can be helpful when the junior faculty members are floundering around looking for research projects and the senior faculty can guide and stimulate them. But when junior faculty members have specific research interests and are "advised" not to pursue them by the senior faculty, academic freedom is just as seriously threatened as when outside control is exerted.

One assistant professor was encouraged by her department to develop and manage a women's studies program in order to increase the number of students registering for the department's courses. She became interested in feminism as a research area and received a contract to write a book on that subject. However, her department decided that this was not a research area that would count for tenure evaluation. With no future in the research area that interested her most, she chose to quit the job and enter another profession. Another assistant professor was told by a senior colleague that it was "inappropriate" for a junior scholar to publish a book presenting a new theory with which the senior professor disagreed. The assistant professor did this anyhow, and his tenure was vigorously opposed by the senior colleague and eventually was denied.

These examples illustrate obvious violations of academic freedom. In many cases the pressure is more subtle. Junior faculty members learn that it is in their professional interest to avoid certain research topics, to stick to traditional areas of research, or to work on a project supervised by a particular colleague. Much advice from senior colleagues is made in good conscience in an attempt to be forthright and specify the conditions they believe necessary or more likely to lead to tenure. Most junior faculty members who choose research topics are quite aware that some choices are more likely to improve the chances for tenure than others, that it is not just the quality of research but the *area* of research that counts for tenure. In other words, they know that they as untenured academics do not have genuine academic freedom.

As we discussed in Chapter 3, the main purpose of the tenure system is to guarantee academic freedom. Once tenure has been granted, the nature of a scholar's beliefs, the direction of research, and the area of publication cannot constitute reason for dismissal. Threat of dismissal is an obvious constraint on research, but in some areas of study academic jobs are not essential to scholarship. Some scholars think of academic jobs as merely a source of income like waiting on tables. In other fields, merely having an academic job is not enough for research; additional funding for equipment and a research team is needed as well. In institutions of higher education the sources of research support include an academic department's budget, the institution's research fund, and grants from foundations, industry, and government agencies. Receiving funds depends on convincing an individual or a committee that the research is more worthwhile than that proposed by competing scholars.

In fields where additional funding is needed for research, the security of tenure is insufficient to guarantee academic freedom. The freedom to work on a subject depends on the priorities of others. Their values and perspectives influence the perception of what should be given priority. The special interests and biases of private and public funding agencies play an important role in determining the direction of research. No one is surprised that the tobacco industry generously supports the Institute for Tobacco and Health, where research on tobacco products is restricted to making their use less harmful to health, or that the American Cancer Society supports research investigating the link between the use of tobacco products and cancer. We expect that oil company foundations will be more likely to fund research to develop a better pollution-control system for gasoline-powered automobiles than research to develop a solar recharging system for electrically powered automobiles. Even within an academic institution there is no policy to guide the head of a psychology department who happens to be a Freudian and has to decide whether to assign the only available research assistant to a colleague who wishes to analyze the content of dreams or to a colleague who wishes to study maze learning in rats.

As we discussed in Chapter 2, one can justify the search for knowledge by saying either that knowledge is a good in itself or that knowledge contributes to other values: making informed choices possible, eliminating suffering, and so on. In either case the *misdirection* of knowledge becomes a serious ethical concern. Therefore, it is important to consider not just the way outside interests, personal jealousies, and scarce resources affect the growth of knowledge but also how the structure of an academic institution, including what its members encourage, reward, respect, or disdain, can foster the search for knowledge.

The system of rewards and punishments discussed in Chapter 3 influences the behavior of researchers. By providing recognition, the esteem of colleagues, and career advancement, the reward system in institutions of higher education affects how research is done. For example, sociologists of science have found that in general, scholars are rewarded more for the quantity of research than for its quality (Cole and Cole 1967). The reward system is arranged so that the average scholar can gain more by trying to maximize the number of publications than by trying to do the best research possible. This system leads to bad consequences of ethical import. Publication, which should be solely a means of disseminating new knowledge, becomes an end in itself. The increased pressure to publish or perish (or at least not flourish) has increased the number of manuscripts submitted to journals and the number of journals as well. Editors have decried the increased tendency for scholars to submit papers just to earn publication credit (Mehler and Bever 1973). Scholars have complained that the publication flood makes it more difficult to find relevant articles and makes it more likely that important research will be missed. Thus, the reward system, by encouraging overpublication, may hinder the dissemination of new knowledge.

In addition to a glut of less significant information, the emphasis on quantity of production rather than quality has the effect of reducing the efficiency and rate of scholarly discovery. In a study designed to clarify the effects of different reward systems on scientific discovery, Robinson (1979) set up a miniature version of the type of scientific research that is conducted in institutions of higher education. He found that reward systems that emphasize quantity over quality tend to slow down the rate at which the larger and more important scientific problems are solved. Another serious danger is that the academic reward system and its pressures will encourage researchers to take shortcuts, use improper research methods, and engage in outright cheating. We shall discuss this in the next section.

Research activities are also influenced by *how* the results are disseminated. Publication in a leading journal has the greatest possible influence, whereas a finding that remains unpublished, is delayed in appearing, or is published in a journal with few readers tends to have little impact on the field. Scholars look to the publication process as a screening device allowing them to sort through only the highest-quality work. Although some scholarly journals and book publishers will publish anything submitted to them (usually for a fee), most editors are more selective. Some scholarly journals report that they reject 98 out of 100 articles submitted to them (Moulton 1975). Publication of research results in such cases becomes a scarce resource, increasing ethical concerns about how to distribute publication space in fair and effective ways.

Many publications are arranged through the Old Boy Network. Book reviews and lead articles are solicited, proceedings of conferences with invited participants are published and editors of anthologies ask their friends to contribute. Ethical problems arise when these practices prevent the publication of better work or allow the publication of inferior work. When much of a journal's space is taken up by the works of its own editorial board, it may be because these people are the best and most prolific in that field. But it is likely that favoritism is being shown to the journal's editors, denying space to others. Famous scholars find that their works are sometimes published with obvious errors overlooked, justifying the suspicion that their submissions are not receiving serious scrutiny.

> Some journal editors have defended favoritism toward the work of famous scholars. They claim that it is important for readers to follow the developing ideas of the leading scholars in the field and that it is newsworthy when great thinkers come up with faulty ideas. Does this justify partiality to famous people?

We can explain editorial favoritism without condoning it. First, since editors believe that scholars are more likely to read articles and books written by leaders in the field, highly regarded scholars are often asked by editors to contribute their work. It is difficult for editors to reject a manuscript they have solicited. Second, there is often a complex process of review and revision that precedes actual publication. Editors may assume that established scholars are more likely to be able to respond to reviewers' criticisms and correct the shortcomings in their submissions. Third, since frequent exposure, independent of quality, tends to create a more favorable impression (Zajonc 1968), a manuscript submitted by a well-published author may have an advantage in terms of first impression. These factors contribute to the kind of catch-22 that raises ethical problems in all fields. Having been published makes it easier to get published. This tends to create a scholarly establishment, making it harder for those outside the established circles to influence the field. The ideal criterion of scholarly merit becomes diluted by pragmatic factors in the publication process. (There are also bits of academic gameship that experienced scholars learn to use deliberately or automatically that may influence manuscript acceptance, such as "flattery citations" of the work of potential reviewers.)

An obvious way to end favoritism toward famous authors as well as other personal biases is to have manuscripts reviewed without knowledge of the author's name or other credentials. Despite pressure from readers and contributors, journal editors in many fields have resisted such "blind" reviewing. In some fields prospective authors can *request* a blind review, but doing so where it is not the general practice marks one as different, alerting reviewers that there is something peculiar about the author. Blind reviewing may help a manuscript by a known and disliked author, but it will not help the unknown author compete with established authors who may be getting preferential treatment.

Favoritism in research publication is unethical, but so is research censorship. Charges of censorship are very serious, but they do occur, particularly when there are strong rival methodologies or views within a field. Let us look at one case where there is no doubt about actual attempts at censorship but where the ethical issues are complex. Immanuel Velikovsky (1950), using anthropological and archeological evidence, made many dramatic claims that certain astronomical events occurred in historical times.

Several established scholars organized a campaign to pressure publishing houses to refuse to accept Velikovsky's works. The campaign included threats to boycott (Goldsmith 1977). This might appear to be a clear case of an attempt to violate the principle of academic freedom to publish and an example of the scholarly establishment squelching the work of a dissident scholar.

However, the established scholars provided strong arguments for not publishing Velikovsky's work. They argued, with good justification as it turned out, that Velikovsky made claims that were not well founded, made so many predictions that some were likely to be true by accident, and cited datas consistent with his thesis while ignoring the inconsistent data (Goldsmith 1977). Because he improperly drew conclusions from weak evidence, his critics argued that publication of Velikovsky's work would do "true" science considerable harm and that his sensational popularizations would misinform the public. Velikovsky's opponents were advancing an argument that considered the consequences and were concluding that publishing his work would do more harm than good. The counterclaim is that preserving the rule of academic freedom is more important than preventing the immediate harm caused by the publication of poorly founded results.

HONESTY IN RESEARCH

The actions that will be considered under this topic lie on a continuum from blatant fraud to ethically suspect practices. In the past several years some cases of research fraud have become so prominent that they have been discussed in the popular press.

When scholars read or hear about the results of another scholar's research, they assume that many aspects of the report can be depended upon: that the data are accurate and complete, that observations are factual and not fictional, and that barring flaws in reasoning, the conclusions can be relied on to the degree of confidence specified in the report. The decision to commit resources of time, effort, and money to a project is often based on previous work in the field. It is a sacred principle of research ethics that one must never knowingly introduce false or misleading information that could possibly subvert or stunt the growth of knowledge.

Although there may be many cases where research is based on false information, it is rare to find a case where the information is deliberately intended to mislead. The "Piltdown man," an archeological fraud in which modern parts were added to an ancient skull to suggest the existence of a human "missing link," is one of the few clear examples where the perpetrators deliberately undermined research (Tullock 1966). Until the fraud was discovered, many archeologists accepted the finding and changed their views of human evolution.

Usually, scholars who violate the principles of research honesty believe in their own hypotheses and do not expect their acts to subvert the course of knowledge. Instead, they subvert the canons of scholarly evidence. They fabricate supporting evidence and distort or suppress contradictory evidence. Unethical scholars behave like crusading district attorneys who want to ensure a conviction for someone they are convinced is guilty and take shortcuts with evidence. There are laws to prevent the introduction of improper evidence in a trial, but there are few safeguards against the introduction of improper evidence in scholarly research.

One famous example of such fraud occurred in the work of Sir Cyril Burt, who presented data that twins brought up in different environments maintained similar IQs. His work was very influential in the development of the British educational system, which decides at an early age which children will have the opportunity of obtaining higher education. It is now believed that Burt fabricated his data on twins in order to show that IQ was genetically determined. There is little doubt that he really believed IQ to be genetically determined and that he did what he thought would convince the public of this "truth."

Sigmund Freud may also have "adjusted" data in order to support first one theory then another. Early in the development of psychoanalysis, Freud presented evidence that children were sometimes the victims of sexual abuse. He argued that these early experiences could cause certain adult neuroses, especially hysteria. Later, as he was developing his theory of the oedipal relationship between parent and child, Freud claimed that such childhood sexual experiences almost never happened but were fantasies invented by his adult patients. However, there is evidence that Freud attended a number of medical examinations of children who were seriously abused. One of his disciples said that this crucial part of psychoanalytic theory might have floundered without the assumption that such abuse was fantasy (Masson 1984).

Scholarly evidence is evaluated according to established standards, especially in science. For example, in the social sciences a scholar must show that data support a hypothesis with at least 95 percent confidence. The purpose of these high standards is to prevent the introduction of a false path into the search for knowledge, something that could mislead hundreds or thousands of researchers and subvert the course of knowledge. There is always the possibility of an error, but the standards of research evidence are designed to keep the risk to a bare minimum. Researchers who violate these standards are secretly taking much higher risks by promoting conclusions from inferior evidence and disguising the quality of that evidence. If the gamble pays off and the claim is sustained, the researcher will get credit for introducing it. If it turns out to be false, not only may the reputation of the scholar suffer, but all subsequent work based on the false conclusion may be subverted. Not only may the knowledge itself be corrupted, so may any applications based on it.

Note that it is not the drawing of conclusions from sparse evidence that is forbidden, only the *false* claim that the evidence is stronger than it actually is. Researchers, like other people, are allowed to state their beliefs and use what prestige, authority, and charisma they have to convince others as long as they do not make false claims about the evidence.

Linus Pauling, a brilliant and respected scientist, became convinced that vitamin C, if taken in sufficient quantity, will prevent colds and other illnesses. The research necessary to prove this claim would take many years and many subjects. He never made any false claims about research, but his influence and reputation gave his claim great publicity. Many people were persuaded to increase their intake of vitamin C before there was any empirical support for the benefit of large doses. In fact, many later studies showed no significant advantage for large doses over the small daily amount recommended by the Food and Drug Administration. Yet many people continue to take large doses of vitamin C. Was Pauling wrong to advocate vitamin C before the research was done? Suppose his claim had been correct? Do researchers who are acknowledged as experts have a special responsibility to be more cautious in their claims than other people?

Research *ethics* and research *methodology* are interrelated and the relationship depends on our understanding of statistics and methodology. For example, consider the act of throwing out data that contradict an experimental hypothesis after a study has been conducted. Today researchers understand that this is both methodologically unsound and, if concealed, ethically unsound.

Not too long ago, throwing out unsupporting data was a common practice among researchers in parapsychology. They believed that extrasensory perception was an ability that only some people had and that these people had it only some of the time. The problem was that the only way to tell who had the ability and when was to look at the results of experiments conducted to support the very existence of ESP. This is like trying to support the hypothesis that a particular roulette wheel is biased toward red but recording only those spins when reds appear. To say that the wheel's ability to produce reds is present only some of the time is not a legitimate justification for this procedure (unless one can specify *before looking at the data* which times red will appear).

Parapsychology researchers usually reported their methods in enough detail so that readers could tell what they had done. But sometimes they disregarded data that contradicted their claims without mentioning it because this was a standard procedure for parapsychology at the time. Is this an ethical or a methodological problem? Can the two be completely separated? Contrast this with the case where a scholar discards information knowing that if it were included, it would weaken or destroy the claim being made.

Changes in research methodology over the ages should be taken into account when we judge the behavior of earlier scholars who have been accused of cheating. The data published by Newton in support of the laws of motion and those published by Mendel in support of the genetic laws of independent assortment have recently been scrutinized (Westfall 1973; Brush 1974; Koestler 1971). In both cases the data are impossibly precise, fitting the theory perfectly but lacking the random variations that were necessarily present in their experiments. It is very clear that Newton and Mendel "neatened up" their data. In the modern perspective, they committed the sin of claiming that their evidence was stronger than it actually was. However, in earlier times the modern conventions of data reporting did not exist. Experiments served as *demonstrations* of theories as well as *tests* of theories. The individual scholar decided whether the results of an experiment supported the theory, and if this was the case, the results were offered as a demonstration of the truth of the theory. Just as the description of a theory was presented in as clear and convincing a way as possible, so also were the results of experiments. This meant that the data could be "cleaned up" just as an equation is cleaned up to appear in the most elegant form.

In recent years several violations of research ethics have received wide publicity. Most of the cases occurred in the sciences, and most of the perpetrators were under a great deal of pressure to produce research findings in quantity. Apparently, all were believers in their own hypotheses and cheated to support their scholarly claims.

John Darsee was the focus of one of the most publicized and troublesome recent cases of research fraud. A prolific and brilliant medical researcher, Darsee was under enormous pressure and was receiving enormous rewards in the form of career advancement and professional acclaim. He believed strongly that his hypothesis about heart disease was correct, so he took shortcuts with his research and reported experiments he had not actually carried out.

Most of the public anger has been focused on Darsee and on his mentor, who listed himself as coauthor of Darsee's papers without actually supervising or even participating in the research (in many laboratory sciences this is a standard practice with its own ethical problems). However, the initial reaction of Darsee's own institution was equally reprehensible. Although the institution was officially absolved from responsibility in the fraud, administrators knew about the fraud and delayed announcing it so that Darsee's "research" continued to be reported to the public for years (Broad 1982a and 1982b).

Research fraud is considered a terrible offense. In theory, it is punished by suspension or expulsion from the profession. It is not a crime against persons or property but against truth. Fraudulent research is often very hard to detect. Scholars are, or should be, skeptical about new findings, but their skepticism is directed at possible flaws in interpretation or methodology, not at the data themselves. Building upon earlier research would be nearly impossible if scholars had to replicate every finding for themselves before trusting it to serve as a basis for new investigations.

It is important to try to get a sense of how commonly research fraud occurs. Is it a very rare event or are the publicized cases just the tip of the iceberg? Students of the problem disagree. Merton (1957) reminds us how strongly originality is stressed in research. In order to be recognized as original, one must be the first to publish a new finding. He admits that this need for priority can pressure some scholars to cut corners in research, but he believes this pressure is so strongly countered by years of training to respect honesty that research fraud is a rare event. In addition, Tullock (1966) and McCain and Segal (1969) emphasize that the danger of being caught, with its severe penalty of expulsion from the field, is a strong deterrent.

On the pessimistic side, Barber (1976) suggests that the type of close replication that is likely to uncover phony data is generally confined to the natural sciences and that fraud is much harder to detect in other research fields. Swazey and Scher (1981) point out that much research in the natural sciences is too expensive to replicate. Remember too that fraud is likely to be detected only when the hypothesis supported by the fudged data is later challenged by other research. Fudged data supporting a correct hypothesis are not likely to be found out.

There are some reasons to be skeptical of Merton's claim that training in higher education inculcates research honesty. Tittle and Rowe (1973) found that 95 percent of 107 students in a sample of three university classes cheated at least once during the semester when they thought they could get away with it. Faber (1974, p. 74) states:

> We are naive to believe that dishonesty in research is unique and aberrant. The rewards are just too tempting: prestige, ego enhancement, promotion, and [financial benefits]. . . . Not only are the rewards tempting but, while the process of socialization in graduate school may give credence to veracity, it nonetheless emphasizes success. The emphasis on scientific success creates a

severe strain on the practicing researcher, who is torn between the norms established for the process of research and the penultimate rewards for success. Under these conditions deviance is likely to occur in any group, even among scientists.

The problem of research fraud is not limited to the sciences. What constitutes fraud is likely to be quite different in other areas: misleading or fictitious quotes and translations, forged letters and diaries, or misdescribed, altered, or misplaced artifacts.

There are a number of recent examples of research fraud in the humanities: fake diaries of Hitler, a false biography of Howard Hughes, plagiarism in best-sellers such as *Roots*. The payoff for these frauds was money (Shaw 1982). Is fraud likely to be less tempting if the payoff is prestige or professional standing? Should punishment for such fraud go beyond professional censure or expulsion to include, as specified in Massachusetts state law (Massachusetts State Legislature 1980), fines or imprisonment?

In summary, research fraud is a serious ethical problem for higher education. It is complicated by many factors: changes and differences in research methodology, the blurry border between a deliberate attempt to deceive one's colleagues and the self-deception that grows out of enthusiasm for one's position, the difficulty in detecting a violation, and the ways in which academic values motivate research fraud.

STEALING IDEAS AND CREDIT

Here are two examples that illustrate how far some academics were willing to go to obtain credit for intellectual achievement.

1.   A graduate student had an idea for a new approach to a problem that he thought would make a very good topic for a doctoral dissertation. He took the plans for the project to his faculty adviser and was encouraged to do the work. Since the adviser was the department expert in the area of his project, the student did not discuss it with any other faculty members. When the project was substantially completed, the adviser told him to stop work in that area and find another dissertation topic because the project "belonged" to the faculty adviser. The faculty adviser published the work under his own name alone. The graduate student, after overcoming his shock, hastily found another (and less interesting) topic, completed the new dissertation, and left the university as soon as he could.

2.   A member of a research team who was gaining prominence over the other members of her team was subjected to severe harassment by jealous

"coworkers." The harassment was so severe—sabotaged research, anonymous threats of bodily harm, and destruction of personal property—that the researcher decided to resign from the project.

Most problems of assigning credit for research occur when two or more people are collaborating on a research project. Publication credit can be roughly ranked as follows:

1. Sole authorship
2. First authorship
3. Joint authorship where alphabetic or other ordering convention is used to assign equal credit.
4. Joint authorship with ranked credit
5. Footnote acknowledgment
6. Unpublished gratitude

It is unfair to receive credit for research out of proportion to one's *intellectual* contribution. This doctrine is formalized in the codes of ethics of some professional organizations. For example, the American Psychological Association (1972, p. 7) requires that authorship be restricted to those who make "major contributions of a professional character." However, this phrase allows great latitude in interpretation so that people can abide by the code but still take credit they do not deserve.

Much research is done jointly. Often the collaboration is across levels of the academic hierarchy: students working as apprentices to the faculty or junior scholars working with senior scholars. There is often an assumption made that knowledge flows from senior scholar to junior scholar, from faculty to student. One might expect a *tendency* for scholarly competence to increase with position in the hierarchy, but scholarly rank is by no means a perfect predictor of the ability to generate and explain new ideas.

Let us look at some of the considerations that affect the assignment of credit. Ideally, it would be clear how much each person contributed intellectually to the project so that credit could be assigned according to the ranking system we have described. In practice, things are much more complicated. Suppose a student who has taken a number of courses with an instructor collaborates with that faculty member on a research project that results in a publishable report. If the student writes a proposal for a research project, it may be hard to determine the extent to which the faculty member was instrumental in providing the intellectual background that led the student to the idea. If a contribution to the background is the only way in which someone participates in a project, this is usually acknowledged in a footnote. Typically, the instructor will also contribute to the research and its reporting at several stages. It may be difficult to figure out when such contributions are more significant than the usual suggestions and criticisms given by one scholar to another so as to be deserving of joint authorship rather than the usual footnote.

It is very common in the sciences for the head of a laboratory or the senior person on a research team to be a joint author of any work done in the lab even when this person has done no work on the particular project or manuscript. In some cases the person is even given first authorship. This common and accepted practice assumes that the senior person has made substantial contributions to the ideas without actually working on their expression. The person may make indirect contributions such as providing laboratory facilities and financial support or lending a famous name to increase the publishability of the results. However, this is not the same as a direct intellectual contribution to the research, and there is something unethical about trading these contributions for research credit.

Taking credit for publications without actually participating in the research can backfire. John Darsee's mentor, Eugene Braunwald, could claim that he enabled Darsee to work in his research area, provided essential laboratory facilities, had occasional but fruitful discussions about the work with him, and was available for advice and help if Darsee wanted it. Because his name appeared on several of the papers written by Darsee, he suffered serious embarrassment and a career setback when it was later discovered that the papers contained fraudulent data (Culliton 1983). Cases like these may help change this practice in the future. In 1983 the American Psychological Association tried to address these concerns by recommending that faculty advisers' names not appear as senior authors on publications deriving from student dissertations (Fields 1983).

The quest for research credit may interfere with the growth of knowledge. Scholars jealously guard access to research materials and keep secret their methodology and preliminary findings so that they cannot be "scooped" by someone else. In one case two different scientists in the same department were working on the same problem in laboratories across the hall from each other. They found out about each other's work only through an outside visitor, not in the same field, who had visited both laboratories. In another case a scholar who had managed to gain an exclusive license to examine a set of antiquities refused for years to share them with others until he had extracted all he could from them.

As long as research credit is central to the distribution of benefits in the academic world, the distribution of research credit will be an ethical problem. We can speculate about the proprietary nature of authorship of research publications and the moral disapproval that attaches to someone who fails to acknowledge someone else's contribution. If the purpose of the work is to increase knowledge, it should not be so important to determine how much each person contributes to the result, but with rare exceptions, authorship credit is treated as a precious commodity. Perhaps this occurs because academics often lose sight of the original goal of knowledge and begin thinking that the main purpose of publishing research is to gain credit and evaluate others. Would the goal of knowledge be better served if institutions of higher education could be changed so that academics paid less attention to authorship and credit and more to the primary purpose of their research efforts?

SUMMARY

In this chapter we examined some of the ethical problems arising from the research conducted in institutions of higher education. We looked at how social, physical, and biological research results are evaluated in terms of ethical consequences. We saw how short-term and long-term consequences are difficult to assess and how inequalities in the distribution of benefits and risks complicate ethical decisions. We talked about how the beneficial consequences of research have to be tempered with consideration for the well-being and dignity of human and animal subjects used in the research. The use of deception in research was examined at some length. Then we discussed how research topics are chosen and pursued and examined the pressures and constraints that impinge on academic freedom. We looked at the influence of the academic reward system, the availability of research funding, pressures on untenured faculty members, and the scholarly publication system in terms of the principles of Fairness, Universalization, and Maximizing Benefits. Next we dealt with the problems of research cheating, considering how research ethics and methodology are intertwined and how conflicts between success and honesty affect the scholar. Finally, we discussed the stealing of credit for research contribution, the safeguards of secrecy, and how the assignment of credit and reward affects the pursuit of knowledge.

Chapter 5

Ethical Problems
in Teaching

Ethical problems that arise in teaching at the level of higher education can be roughly divided into five areas:

1. *Who* to teach: issues in admissions, recruiting, and flunking out
2. *What* to teach: depth, breadth, bias, and freedom of choice
3. Evaluating students: "subjective" and "objective" criteria
4. Student cheating: plagiarism and term paper services
5. Professor-student relations: misuses of power and influence

WHO TO TEACH

In several places in this book we have discussed how scarcity of resources creates or worsens ethical problems for institutions of higher education. Either of the two main commodities of college admissions—places in the entering class and students to fill those places—can become scarce. We shall first look at some of the ethical issues raised when a place in the entering class is the scarce commodity and then examine situations where there are not enough students to fill the entering class.

In most states of the United States and in many other countries the public commitment to provide education for all citizens ends with graduation from high school. Colleges that have more applicants than openings try to select the "best" possible group of people for their entering classes. This selection process involves some interesting ethical problems.

Almost all institutions of higher education require their applicants to be high school graduates. For some colleges this may be sufficient for admission, but many institutions require more: good grades, teacher recommendations, extracurricular accomplishments, and high scores on aptitude and achievement tests. Some schools require certain religious affiliations or congressional nominations as well, and many schools have age restrictions. Some of these restrictions are motivated by academic values. With selective admissions, the students admitted are more likely to have similar abilities, preparation, and intellectual interests. Without background skills and information, many topics are impossible to learn. If the pace of courses is slowed by students who need remedial explanations, better students become bored and frustrated. With a more demanding pace, the less able students will get low grades or fail, and this can be demoralizing on a large scale.

However, selective admission does prevent many people from getting a chance to study at the better schools, thereby denying equal opportunity to gain an important means of future status and power in the society. Considerations of fairness and equal opportunity are modulated by meritocratic academic values. The ethical compromise is further complicated by the difficulty of assessing scholarly potential. Aptitude tests do only a fair job of predicting future performance. More subjective criteria, such as evaluating essays and impressions at interviews, depend heavily on the individuals who do the evaluating. For example, many interviews are conducted by alumni, some of whom may have old-fashioned ideas about the sort of student the school should accept. Since admission decisions are based on such rough predictors of future performance, some people who could do the work are prevented from having a chance.

If we used aptitude tests and interviews to decide who was a potential criminal and then prevented some people from free access to society because of their performance, it would seem to be unfair. Yet we deny many people access to a high-level education on the basis of similar judgments. Compare these cases. Nighttime curfews on young people and higher insurance rates on the basis of age and sex are controversial because they also involve restrictions on the basis of membership in high-risk groups. Does the morality of differential treatment depend on how group membership is defined?

Public universities, which are supported by tax money and run by the state or federal government, have more difficulty justifying restricted admissions than privately funded schools. Some schools have tried "open" admissions, allowing anyone with a high school diploma to enroll. This means that there are large differences in the educational backgrounds and abilities of the students who are accepted. Either the school must lower its standards, teaching less more thoroughly and giving higher grades for lesser work, or many of the students will fail. If the school lowers its standards, it provides an inferior education and an inferior credential to its students. If the school flunks out large numbers of students, it has allowed students to invest time and money under the false hope that they could pass. The latter policy has often been justified by claims that it maximizes fairness and equal opportunity. Looked at another way, open admissions can be seen as abdicating the responsibility to make necessary judgments, reflecting an unwillingness to take on the unpleasant and sometimes politically unpopular task of telling applicants that they do not have the background or ability to do the work.

For many colleges the most prominent factor in admission decisions is intellectual aptitude, which includes all the abilities and background a student can use to learn and to increase knowledge. But admission decisions are not based on intellectual aptitude alone. Other factors that influence these decisions can raise ethical problems.

Colleges describe their admissions selection criteria stressing intellectual aptitude, but they frequently mention other attributes as well. They want students who are well rounded, mature, creative, assiduous, and socially aware. If a college announces to applicants that some particular set of criteria forms the basis for admission decisions, it would be unfair to use other criteria that are not made public. Yet there often are other criteria for admission that a college is not willing to announce. Some colleges have had admission "quotas" based on ethnic or racial membership. For example, Jews, often identifiable by surname, were sometimes denied admission in favor of less qualified applicants (Baltzell 1964). Today admission quotas are considered unjust and morally reprehensible, analogous to the legal bill of attainder, and designed to restrict access to an important resource by discriminating on an illegitimate basis.

Let us consider restrictions on college admissions that are similar in some respects to the old racial and ethnic quotas. Several coeducational institutions have quotas for the number of women they admit. One reason given for this practice is that dormitory space is available only for a limited number of women, that bathrooms are equipped with urinals and too few toilets to meet building codes for female occupancy, that women expect individual showers in place of communal shower rooms, and that remedying these inadequacies would be prohibitively expensive. These arguments have been challenged by lawsuits and federal legislation.

Suppose a school decides to admit 51 percent women. Is this still a quota system? Why or why not? We can imagine a rationale for such a policy: balancing to reflect the proportion of women in the population. But are such rationales legitimate? Does your answer depend on what you think the percentage of women admitted would be if there were no such policy?

How do the sex quotas of a coeducational institution compare with the admissions policies of colleges that restrict access entirely to people of one sex? Institutions educating only one sex have a very long tradition: schools controlled by religious bodies, the historical exclusion of women from most secular educational institutions, and later the establishment of women's seminaries and colleges. Many traditional single-sex colleges decided to change their policy so that by 1981 more than 96 percent of accredited senior colleges and universities in the United States were coeducational (Dolmatch 1981). But there are still some distinguished schools (e.g., Smith, Wellesley, and Mount Holyoke Colleges) that continue to restrict admission to one sex. Let us look at the arguments for and against this restriction.

Even after it became generally acceptable for women to gain access to higher education, proponents of single-sex education claimed that separation of the sexes would avoid the distractions of heterosexual romance. This is still a central reason given for maintaining all-male schools, most of which are religious seminaries. For all-female schools another argument is given: Because men are dominant in our culture, a college devoted totally to the education of women provides a place where women more easily learn to recognize their own excellence and can command the attention and respect of other scholars instead of taking the second place they often do in a coeducational school. Furthermore, women will be less influenced by sex stereotyping in choosing courses of study and therefore are more likely to choose majors that are predominantly chosen by men in coeducational institutions. Data support this position. For example, the proportion of women students becoming professional scientists is higher among graduates of women's colleges (Conway 1977), even though better science faculty and facilities are available at some coeducational universities.

Since access to a higher education is a valuable benefit, the exclusion of men on the basis of sex seems to be unfair. However, the exclusion of men is argued for on the grounds that the benefit to women outweighs the harm done to men by excluding them from particular educational resources. This argument is reflected in court decisions that have dismissed claims for the admission of men to women's colleges, concluding that student populations may be restricted where there is an overriding concern for providing a specialized education for a particular group, such as schools for the handicapped, remedial education, and so on (Thomas 1983). In effect, supporters of women's colleges are arguing that women are educationally handicapped in the environment of a coeducational school because of current social values. Providing a resource for this group is a benefit that overrides a strict interpretation of the Principle of Fairness.

Admissions criteria are often modified in order to increase the *diversity* of the student population. Diversity is commonly achieved by using geographical location as a basis on which to vary the people admitted. The argument in favor of diversity is that knowing and learning about people with different backgrounds is an important part of an education. The experience of working with a variety of people is valuable, and their diverse backgrounds, values, and presuppositions contribute to the intellectual growth the college tries to foster. This claim is related to the arguments for diversity in faculty that were discussed in Chapter 3. Although it achieves this benefit, the use of diversity to modify selection criteria does cause inequalities in applying the main admissions criteria: People, who happen to belong to groups with larger numbers of applicants have to meet higher standards. The goal of maximizing the benefits of diversity for students and other members of the institution requires equal treatment for some applicants with unequal "intellectual" qualifications.

Suppose Terry has better qualifications for admission to college than Chris, but Terry is from an area with a high density of college-preparatory high schools whereas Chris is from a rural area where few young people apply to college. Chris may be favored over Terry in college admissions because Chris will add to the geographical diversity of the student body. Is this fair? Terry had better grades, more advanced courses, and higher aptitude test scores than Chris, probably because Terry had the advantage of a better precollege education in the first place. What counts as equal opportunity in this case?

Geographical diversity can be abused as a criterion. One dean at an Ivy League university strongly supported geographical diversity because in reducing the number of students from large cities with large populations of racial and ethnic minorities, he was able to increase the proportion of what he called "real Americans" on campus.

In contrast, many colleges make a deliberate effort to modify the main admissions criteria in order to increase racial, ethnic, and socioeconomic diversity. They assume that the institution has a social responsibility to distribute the benefits of a higher education to groups in which they are scarce and would make a significant impact on the general welfare of the group.

However, the morality of attempts to increase diversity has been challenged. In 1974 Allan Bakke sued the University of California regents because he was denied admission to medical school. He argued that admissions criteria were applied unfairly since his credentials were better than those of some minority group members who were actually admitted. The case went to the United States Supreme Court, which found the particular method of favoring minority applicants used by the school unlawful but upheld the school's "according . . . consideration to race in its future admission policy" (United States Supreme Court Reports, V. 57).

Favoring ethnic and geographical diversity is not the only admissions policy that may conflict with fairness and equal opportunity. Many schools favor applicants who are relatives of alumni, asking prospective students to list alumni relatives on admission applications. One defense of this policy is that being the relative of someone who graduated from the college is a kind of credential. Such a candidate is more likely to have been raised in a family that has intellectual and other values compatible with those of the college. The candidate is more likely to know about, be able to get along in, and appreciate the particular college environment because a family member was a student there. Furthermore, students may be more motivated to do well if backed by a family tradition.

Another defense is that the school owes something to alumni and that preferential treatment of their offspring is repayment. Although the nature of such an obligation may be unclear, another reason for partiality is closely related: Donations are more likely to come from alumni who feel strong ties of loyalty to their college, and loyalty is more likely to be strong toward a college that serves as alma mater to several people in a family. Fairness in admissions opportunity is compromised here because most colleges depend on the money from alumni contributions.

In the early 1980s it became public knowledge that some colleges recruited athletes who were academically unprepared for college, forged their transcripts, and kept them enrolled until their playing eligibility was used up even though many received no educational benefits and were not granted a degree. Should a college ever recruit students who fail to meet the academic standards? If it does, should they be given remedial training and special tutoring to help them get through their courses? Should athletic recruits be treated like other students and flunked out if they cannot do the work? Could the faculty teaching star athletes or the offspring of wealthy donors face an ethical dilemma if it is important for the economic health of the college that such students pass regardless of the quality of their work?

In the early 1960s colleges expanded rapidly to accommodate the increased number of high school graduates of the "baby boom" that followed World War II. After the early 1960s the birthrate declined, reducing the number of people who later applied to college. Increasing costs and decreasing financial aid have also reduced the number of applicants. The combination of dwindling financial resources and fewer young people of college age has produced a situation in which many colleges are having trouble recruiting students to fill their entering classes. Some have undergone large reductions in staff and facilities, and others have had to close. Several colleges are responding to the new situation with energetic campaigns of advertising and recruiting.

Even schools that attract very good students because their reputations discourage all but the best applicants may be hurt if they accept a large *percentage* of applicants. Many high school advisers and college guidebooks take a high acceptance ratio as a sign that a school does not have the highest-quality students. Therefore, schools are under great pressure to encourage more students to apply—even if they are unqualified—in order to maintain the public image of a highly selective school.

One good effect is that a broader range of people are now encouraged to become college students: retired people, people who did not finish college when they were younger, people interested in changing careers, and people who have completed the most demanding period of raising a family. With such a long tradition of colleges accepting applicants directly from high school, older people rarely have considered themselves eligible.

However, a new source of ethical problems arises in the competition for students. Each student provides a source of money for the college that becomes more important as other sources diminish. Besides direct monies from tuition, state-supported institutions are often funded in proportion to the number of students enrolled. As a result some institutions are admitting large numbers of students who are marginally or not at all prepared for college education. Unable to provide the remedial training necessary, these colleges relax their grading and graduation standards and increase class sizes because their budgets for teaching personnel are usually reduced at the same time, all in order to stay alive financially. The college's viability becomes the main end in itself, and the very students who are supposed to be a major *reason* for the college's existence become the *means*. The college compromises its educational mission in order to continue to exist. Students are cheated because they learn less, and the time they spend may result in a degree that is a worthless credential. Treating students as means for the continued existence of an institution is defended by saying that the survival of the institution will benefit more people in the long run. Claims about potential consequences may be questionable, but even if they are correct, it is not clear that they justify these actions.

Is it morally right for a school to adopt a policy of admitting many students, collecting their tuition money, and then allowing a large proportion of them to flunk out? A number of prestigious schools are proud of such policies, touting them as indications of their high standards. What effects do such policies have on students? Do students become more competitive, more anxious, learn more? Are students proud to belong to such a school? Are such policies fair to students? Do they increase benefits? Do they exploit students for the college's reputation?

WHAT TO TEACH

In founding the university named after him, Ezra Cornell said that he wished to establish an institution "where any person can find instruction in any study" (Cornell 1982). Of course, no college can provide such an unlimited curriculum because there are too many subjects. Perhaps no college should even be willing to offer instruction in any subject. Some things are more worth teaching than others. The choices made in this departure from Ezra Cornell's ideal raise interesting ethical questions. Colleges frequently specialize in certain kinds of education. One college will stress mathematics, science, and engineering while another stresses humanities. Even within specialized institutions the educational emphasis varies. For example, one law school will stress legal theory and philosophy, and another will train students primarily to be expert legal practitioners. In Chapters 2 and 4 we looked at how the relationship of the institution to society affects the topics chosen for research and teaching. Here we want to examine some of the decisions about the curriculum that occur within a college.

A college degree is a credential that conveys a set of expectations that the holder has reached a certain level of intellectual competence, proficiency, and judgment. It is a required credential for many jobs and for graduate and professional schools. But what does the granting of a degree actually say about the graduate? What can one expect of the holder?

In the past, most liberal arts colleges had requirements designed to assure that each student took courses in a number of different subjects as well as specializing in a major area. The curriculum was supposed to provide "breadth and depth." Each major area had its own set of required courses to ensure that the field was studied in sufficient depth. Breadth was enforced by *distribution requirements* that worked like the family dinner menu in Chinese restaurants: "two each from columns A, B, and C and one from column D," where A, B, C, and D were likely to specify foreign languages, science courses, English composition, and so on. The idea was to provide all students with a broad, or "liberal," education, enabling them to appreciate and manage many facets of life. A liberal education was thought to be essential for being a good citizen. A liberal arts degree attested to the holder's wide range of competence. An employer could expect the holder of a liberal arts degree from a good college to read correspondence in French or German, appreciate the art and architecture in the company headquarters, understand the delicacy of the company's negotiations to sell cameras in Saudi Arabia, and be a wise and witty guest at business dinners.

Colleges that constrain their students' courses of study believe that students who are permitted to elect any program of study may graduate with serious deficiencies in important academic areas. But required courses present problems. Many teachers find it unpleasant to teach students who are forced to take their courses and who may be uninterested and uninspiring. Jealously and resentment are directed against departments controlling required courses that guarantee them large numbers of students. New subjects and fields of study require collegewide curriculum changes that take time and bureaucratic maneuvering. Also, the appearance of new areas of study (cognitive science and black studies, for example) suggests that there is no fixed list of topics that constitute a liberal education. Therefore, many colleges have relaxed or eliminated their distribution requirements, allowing students greater freedom to choose their courses of study. The college's role is then limited to making available those courses of study which it considers valuable. Aside from the argument that students should handle the responsibility for their own education, the rationale is that today's culture is so varied and complex that the old program of one kind of liberal education for everyone is no longer appropriate.

A number of ethical questions are involved in the debate about how much the college should control its students' programs of study. One problem is analogous to a central issue in child raising: Does a more experienced person who knows more about the consequences of following or failing to follow a course of behavior have either the right or the responsibility to constrain the choices of someone who cannot know the consequences as well? College educators are more likely to have a better appreciation of the value of particular college subjects than students who have little idea of the material covered or the ways in which a course may be useful as preparation for graduate training or a career.

When the person facing the consequences is a child or a mentally incompetent person, it seems ethically correct for responsible parents or guardians to constrain the choices of the child or ward. Since the chooser is incapable of fully appreciating the consequences, the basis for the choice is incomplete. This principle is similar to the qualification of the Principle of Informed Consent for research subjects discussed in Chapter 4. In complex modern cultures the principle is extended to competent adults in realms where most citizens could not be expected to know fully the consequences of their actions. For example, building codes constrain our choice of construction materials and methods, and food and drug regulations restrict our choice of products to ingest. The rationale for these restrictions is that only an expert can fully appreciate the consequences of decisions made in these realms.

> Should college students be considered children with respect to their ability to select their own programs of study? Even if they are considered adults, is the selection of a study program one of those realms where there is a sufficient danger of harmful consequences so that a "responsible party" has the duty or right to constrain their choices?

Whether a college requires students to take certain courses or merely makes the courses available, there remains the important question of how these courses are selected. Political, social, and economic pressures may influence the nature and development of a college curriculum. For example, during World War II it was nearly impossible to get a new course on German literature or culture approved in American colleges; sentiment against the Nazi regime strongly colored the evaluation of anything German, and many existing courses on German literature and culture were dropped. Years later we can see that the works of Goethe, Beethoven, and Kant did not suddenly diminish in value, but that was not the way it was seen in the 1940s. Economic pressures on college students to have marketable skills by the time they graduate influence which colleges and courses students choose. Colleges in turn adjust their curricula to meet these demands. For example, computer science curricula have expanded while classics curricula have been frozen or even reduced. Cherishing academic freedom, educators may complain about not wanting "vocational" considerations to control the subject matter taught in their schools. But with increased competition for students, few colleges can afford to be completely independent from trends of student interest.

Course requirements create serious concern in many colleges. Textbook selection and the choice of readings for courses may have even greater moral effects but have not been given the same attention. Censorship in high school texts is common because these texts are usually chosen by school committees that want to keep young students from political and religious controversy, sexual information, and moral issues (Kahane 1984).

Higher education is supposed to teach one to think for oneself, to question accepted views and consider alternatives. College teachers are not told by school committees what to teach. In most cases college teachers choose the readings assigned in their courses and the topics that are covered. Apart from some pressure to include standard subject matter in introductory courses and perhaps to use a textbook written by a colleague, they are free to teach what they want. Often a new course *description* has to be approved by a committee, but it is rare that anyone checks to see if a college teacher is following the course description listed in the catalog. This freedom is part of academic freedom, but it is freedom for the instructor, not the students. College teachers, like other people, are biased, opinionated, and eager to convert others to their own views. Every college teacher who selects readings and topics for a course is in effect censoring by selecting some things and excluding others. In many cases the only exposure a student will have to some topics is what is given in a college course. Selection of material carries weight because it is made by an expert, and students may not be exposed to other sources of information on the topic. Many college instructors believe that they can present the facts impartially without including any values. We have already discussed how this is impossible.

Textbook authors also select material on the basis of their own values. The instructor may supplement a text with other readings or ignore some parts of a text, but in many courses, particularly introductory survey courses in which most students have had little other experience with the subject matter, the material included in a textbook is very influential. If we think that fairness requires an equal presentation of all sides of a controversial subject, this pattern conflicts with academic freedom and academic values. Academic freedom allows authors and teachers to select whatever *they* consider worthwhile. Academic values encourage each instructor to decide what material is correct, interesting, worthwhile, or intellectually profound. One side of a controversial issue is likely to be slighted or criticized.

In an effort to include references to women in an introductory philosophy anthology, the editor included a dialog between René Descartes and Elizabeth of Bohemia. They did, in fact, carry on a correspondence around 1643 in which they often discussed philosophical issues. But the dialog—called "The Princess and the Philospher," not "Two Philosophers" (Vesey 1981)—is not at all like their correspondence. In his actual letters Descartes always addressed Elizabeth, whose status was higher than his, as "Your Highness," but in the fictional account this is overlooked. Instead, she addresses him as "Master." In reality they discussed philosophy; in fiction Descartes is the teacher, Elizabeth the student. The dialog is salted with stage directions for Elizabeth (interrupting, indignant, impatiently, continues puzzled, rummages) that undermine her comments in contrast to Descartes' directions (pensively, animated, slowly and emphatically). The dialog begins with some presumptuous sexual flattery by Descartes that would have been as inappropriate in reality as if it had been said by Mick Jagger to Queen Elizabeth II. Neither the editor of the anthology nor the publisher was bothered by these distortions of history, even though students could be seriously misled by the dramatization.

PROBLEMS IN EVALUATING STUDENTS

Grades are very important to most students. They serve as an evaluative summary of a student's experience and as a credential for scholarship support, admission to graduate or professional school, and jobs. Most ethical problems about grades are problems about fairness.

Grading has aspects that may not promote either ethical or academic values. People may be reluctant to try new areas of learning if they are going to be graded. Some of the most important learning experiences—the questioning of fundamental values, "aha!" experiences, and soul-searching events—may not be appropriate to grade. Grading enhances rather than lessens differences in power. Great differences in power between individuals strain moral relations and prevent the free exchange of ideas that is important to the development of knowledge.

Yet in many cases grading is appropriate, if only to provide feedback, maintain academic standards, and provide credentials. Therefore, we must take a closer look at the basis for assigning grades.

One issue is whether a grade should reflect only the past performance of the student, achievement in the course, or whether it should also be a prognostic credential that provides an indication of how well that student is likely to do in future courses, in graduate school, or in a job. Grades that are mainly intended to reflect performance are based directly on examples of the student's work. Grades that are mainly intended to be prognostic may involve additional subjective judgments. This greater leeway in subjective judgment, although it can provide more useful information, does increase the possibility of unfairness in the evaluation process. Moreover, a grade based on performance provides students with more information about the basis for grading, and this can be important in terms of giving students freedom and options in a situation where others have power over them.

Another issue is whether the standards for grading should depend on the performance of others in the class. Should the grades be "curved" or not? Some instructors claim that they have independent standards of competence and that it is therefore possible for every student in a class to get an A (or an F). Others would argue that a totally independent standard is not possible or useful and that grades are most meaningful as a measure of the relative competence of students compared with their peers.

Grading on a curve means that one's grade depends not just on one's own performance but on how others do in the class. Although such a policy assures that the proportion of high grades available will remain constant from year to year, it is likely to increase competitiveness among students. What are the ethical consequences of increasing competitiveness among classmates? What effect does grade curving have on the primary purpose of teaching—increasing students' intellectual abilities and knowledge?

An issue related to grade curving is whether a course grade should depend on how much or how little the student has *improved* during the course or depend on *absolute* measures of ability. If grades are a measure of improvement, they can provide motivation by acting as rewards and punishments for all students, from the most competent through the least able. Supporters of this system claim that it encourages every student to work hard and get the most benefit from the educational institution. Furthermore, native intelligence and previous knowledge are not themselves rewarded so that students will not be afraid to take courses in areas that are new to them. Students eager to get good grades will not be tempted to restrict their courses to subjects they already know something about.

Crtitics argue that this sytem has too many disadvantages. First, it lessens the value of grades as predictors of future performance. Second, it fails to give an indication of the student's performance relative to other students.

Third, it is unfair to those who do well from the beginning and hence do not show as much improvement. Fourth, it may discourage good performance in the beginning of a course, making it subject to abuse by students who may find it to their advantage to hold back in the beginning in order to show greater improvement.

A related question is whether effort and hard work per se should be rewarded independently of the amount accomplished. Students often feel that their grades ought to reflect how much time they spend on their work, and sometimes they appeal for a higher grade on this basis. Many instructors are sympathetic to this position; since effort is usually required for good work, it seems reasonable to encourage students to work hard. An opposing view claims that it is essential in higher education to teach people how to recognize and do *high-quality* work and that rewarding for effort independently of quality thwarts this central goal.

Because of the potential importance of grades, students are rightly concerned with how they are determined. How a grade is computed used to be entirely up to the instructor. Examination scores, papers, and class participation might contribute in either a formal or an informal way to the final grade. Some instructors had clear formulas for determining grades, and some did not. The individual instructor still chooses the basis for grading, but now there is a tendency for instructors to make the method for computing course grades explicit and public. The new system gives students more knowledge of how their grades are determined and therefore more control over their fate. Many instructors and many collegewide policies have now given up the old attitude of "just learn well for the sake of learning and your grade will take care of itself." Now, in many colleges and courses, students have demanded and received the right to know in advance how each piece of work they do will contribute to the grade. In some courses there is a written contract made between student and instructor. The idea is to reduce the possibility for unfairness and error in grade assessment.

Central to the issue of fairness in grade determination is the difference between "objective" and "subjective" criteria. The multiple choice examination and those courses where the final grade is determined by averaging multiple choice exams seem to provide clear examples of objective grading. The grading of an oral performance and the evaluation of "class participation" seem to be clear examples of subjective grading. Although they are impossible to use for some material, many people believe that objective tests—formalized, precise evaluations—are the ideal. Subjective evaluations depend on the instructor's attitude as well as the student's performance. Different instructors, or the same instructor at different times, may have different attitudes toward the same or equivalent performances.

However, the selection and wording of objective exam questions can introduce the same problems that worry us about subjective grading. Here are some examples.

1.   An instructor in a general psychology course whose specialty is physiological psychology selects a higher proportion of questions from that area. As a result, students who are interested and better prepared in that area have an advantage. Since these students do better in the course, they are more likely to register for other courses with this instructor. Instructors are usually pleased to have students interested in their specialties, and high enrollments may even have a positive effect on tenure and promotion decisions. The bias for selecting physiological questions for exams need not be deliberate on the part of the instructor; since the instructor chose to specialize in that area, it is natural that this subject matter is valued more than that of other areas.

2.   A political science instructor uses examples in her exam questions that depend on some knowledge of California state politics. Students from that state have a natural advantage; not only are they likely to know things that will help them answer the questions, they may feel more comfortable with the "homey" examples.

3.   A test that is used to assess reasoning ability requires students to solve analogies. However, some of the vocabulary words used in the test, such as *codicil, debenture, ketch,* and *niblick,* are more likely to be familiar to members of the middle and upper socioeconomic classes. The wording of the test, therefore, makes it partly a test of exposure to the world of wealth and leisure rather than a test of reasoning ability alone.

4.   A student of average ability happens to enroll in a particular course during a term when several very talented students are also enrolled. Although the tests are all objective, the instructor decides to "curve" the final grades. As a result the average student receives a much lower grade than he or she would have received if the group of very talented students had not enrolled.

5.   There is always the possibility of making an error in the scoring and summing of an objective examination. Imagine a final examination (that is not returned to the students) on which an instructor adds the scores on one paper incorrectly so that the grade turns out to be much lower than it should be. If the exam belongs to a student the instructor respects highly, there is a good chance the instructor will be surprised at the low score and check the addition. If the instructor does not think highly of the student, the low grade is not surprising, and the scoring is less likely to be corrected.

Thus, even what seems to be the most objective grading procedure is not without subjective elements. The actual scoring of an exam may be strictly formalized, but the selection of the questions cannot be. In some fields an adequate multiple choice exam would be extremely difficult or impractical to construct. But subjectivity may not be all bad. The danger is that irrelevant factors that are unfair to the student will influence the judgment. But irrelevant factors (for example, distracting noise or an overheated room) may affect performance on an objective test as well. Subjective judgments may even be able to compensate for irrelevant factors, for example, in the case of an instructor who ignores the grade on an examination for a student who has just experienced a personal tragedy.

The real problem is that grading may be influenced by irrelevant factors. In order to be fair, judgments must be made using relevant criteria and must not be influenced by irrelevant factors. It may be impossible for people to prevent irrelevant factors from having *some* effect on a complex judgment. Moral problems become serious when the irrelevant factors are the result of some bias on the part of the instructor. As evaluation becomes less formalized, leaving more to the judgment of the instructor, there is more opportunity for bias to affect the grade. At best, instructors can try to be alert to biases and deliberately try to counteract their effects on judgment.

Let us consider two forms of bias: systematic and unsystematic. Systematic bias occurs when an instructor dislikes a student either as an individual or as a member of a group (racial, ethnic, sexual, or political) and yields to the natural tendency to see more readily the faults and less readily the good points in the performance of that student. Recognizing the problem, many instructors deliberately try to overcome their prejudice, but this is very difficult to do. Some instructors claim that they probably overcompensate and are likely to give students they dislike higher grades than they otherwise deserve. One solution to this problem would be for instructors to grade without knowing whose work they are looking at. But this, like objective testing, is sometimes impossible. Handwriting, style, subject matter, and personal references limit the effectiveness of grading "blind." In addition, some evaluations cannot be done blind, such as an oral defense of a thesis or a seminar presentation. Some instructors feel that grading blind eliminates valuable information. If they know who it is, they can understand better what was intended in an essay, for example. But this may also be a source of unfairness. For example, a brilliant essay written by a student thought to be mediocre may well be devalued and given a lower grade.

Unsystematic biases are more insidious and harder to guard against. One form occurs when an instructor grades one student's work afer grading another's. The effect of an average piece of work read right after a brilliant one is diminished by contrast, whereas it would be augmented if it were read after a real clunker. The mood of the grader may have an effect as well. Imagine the effect of a student's sympathetic short story about a character resembling the instructor's ex-spouse, rebellious offspring, or inconsiderate neighbor. It takes a lot of effort to reduce unsystematic bias. An instructor may read papers more than once in different random orders, or two or more graders may read each piece of work. Since unsystematic bias may be negative or positive at random, the chances of a single student being seriously hurt are small. However, unsystematic biases can accumulate and have a significant effect on the grades of a very few students.

> A conscientious instructor of a large course made up new questions for every multiple choice examination. Recognizing that it was always possible for some unanticipated ambiguity or some vagueness in the lectures to be responsible for misunderstandings, he did an "item analysis," eliminating from the grading any question that was missed by most of the students who got over 90 percent of the rest of the exam correct. One student who had failed the exam complained. It turned out that if certain questions had not been eliminated, this student would have passed. Did the student have a legitimate complaint? Is item analysis ethically sound?

Grade inflation seems to have accompanied economic inflation, bringing with it comparable problems. Many years ago it was common for instructors to reserve the grade of A for work of exceptional quality. Now an A grade is commonly given for a "good" performance. One or two A grades in a class of twenty-five used to be standard; now in many classes of that size ten or more A grades are awarded. Since grades have become very important for postgraduate situations, students often pressure faculty members to raise their grades. Students may challenge low grades, ask for justification, request make-up exams and additional work to raise their grades, and so on. Instructors try to avoid such time-consuming and emotionally upsetting complaints. Other pressures include student comments on course evaluation forms and the pleasant experience of handing back high rather than low grades. Many instructors suspect (whether or not it is actually true) that giving higher grades makes them more popular teachers, increases course enrollment, and reduces the frequency of complaints to their colleagues. When the teaching ability of junior faculty members is evaluated, course evaluations, enrollment figures, and complaints from individual students are likely to make a strong impression. Junior faculty members whose professional survival is at stake may easily give in to this pressure; some may not even be aware they are doing this.

Grade inflation also occurs because instructors and schools do not want to put their students at a disadvantage in competing with other students. Like inflation of the monetary system, the effect increases the cause, making it very difficult to stop the upward trend. Analogously, grade inflation reduces the value of all grades. Also, since only the upper end of the scale is used, grades become less effective in distinguishing levels of quality. Trying to favor one's own students by giving them nominally high grades can be a disservice, misrepresenting student abilities so that unprepared and incompetent people are placed in positions of trust and responsibility. The ethical problem with grade inflation, as with other forms of inflation, is the time scale over which benefits are weighed. Grade inflation may have short-term benefits, but it results in long-term harm.

CHEATING

In Chapter 4 we described the pressures on college faculty that lead to cheating in research. Many of the same career pressures also apply to students. Since grades rather than research publications are the student's main credential, gaining higher grades is the motivation for cheating.

Cheating is an interesting kind of moral infraction. It is the gaining of something undeserved and the false representation of one's abilities or accomplishments. Considering each (successful and undiscovered) act of cheating in isolation, it is difficult to justify its elimination merely by weighing the total immediate harms and benefits. It often provides a large benefit to the cheater and at the same time does not *directly* harm any other person or persons. All other students in the system may suffer a tiny bit because the value of their grades is diminished slightly by the resulting grade inflation, but the harm done to the other individuals involved may be so small that it will have no real effect on their lives. There is, of course, the possibility of indirect *consequential* harm both to the cheater and to others. By avoiding the experience required to attain the grade properly, the cheater may be handicapped by the missing skill or knowledge. Imagine an air force cadet cheating on an eye examination and then failing to see a commercial airliner on a training flight. More subtly, cheaters may harm their own sense of self-worth when they realize that they are not really qualified for the credential they cheated to gain.

Arguments against cheating that weigh costs and benefits are usually based on the Principle of Universalization. What if everyone did it? If cheating were common, two serious problems would arise: The basic relationship of trust between faculty and students would disappear, and grades would become meaningless because one could never tell when a grade measured what it was supposed to. Arguments based on the Golden Rule are similar in terms of the relationships of the cheater to other students and to their instructors. Potential cheaters would not want others to cheat because this would put *them* at a relative disadvantage because other students' cheating would lower the value of the potential cheaters' grades. Of course, students would not want to be cheated by their instructors. Ethical theories that do not explain right and wrong in terms of consequential costs and benefits would say that cheating is wrong because it gains by deception something that one is not entitled to; it is therefore unjust.

There are many forms of cheating, ranging from sneaking a look at a neighbor's exam paper to the changing of grades on school computer records (made famous in the movie *War Games*). Two forms—plagiarism and "term paper research" services—involve interesting ethical questions.

Plagiarism is defined as appropriating someone else's words or ideas without acknowledging that person's contribution. It is a serious form of cheating because not only does one unfairly get credit for something one has not done, one also deprives the original authors of the credit that is rightly theirs. Students are not the only ones who commit this offense. A major university was seriously embarrassed when it was discovered that the inaugural speech of its new president contained passages lifted from the work of another person.

Students understand that it is wrong to copy the text of another author, but a more problematic form of plagiarism occurs when *ideas* are stolen without appropriating the author's actual wording. The theft of ideas without their original wording is hard to discover, hard to prove, and easier to commit without deliberate awareness; it can be crime without intent. It also is more difficult to appreciate the seriousness of this kind of plagiarism and more difficult to learn what counts as a stolen idea since this is a concept that may differ from field to field (Canuteson 1983).

Scholars, whether student or faculty, often read or hear about subjects they are doing, or will do, research on. Unless they are taking careful notes that are later used in composing their own papers, they often digest the material and fail to remember where they learned it. Research on human information processing suggests that this occurs regularly (Kelman and Hovland 1953). When scholars do their own writing on the subject, they may use some of these ideas without being aware that they got them from someone else. An act of plagiarism has certainly occurred, but whether the act is immoral and whether the unaware plagiarist should be held responsible are more difficult questions. (Notice that this problem is similar to the problem of assigning credit for research that was discussed in Chapter 4.)

High school students often believe that plagiarism occurs only when one copies word for word from the writing of another. They learn that one should use quotation marks and citation credit for any direct quotation from another author but not that the original author must be given credit even if the specific wording is changed. Sometimes college students make the same error. For example, the brochure setting out the honor code of a prestigious liberal arts college uses examples suggesting that plagiarism consists only of uncredited direct quotation, and it permits faculty members to "waive restrictions concerning crediting of sources."

What counts as plagiarism depends on subtleties of research methodology and on what counts as an intellectual contribution in each field. Philosphers often use someone else's colorful example without credit. Some of the examples are so classic and famous that they need no credit; their originators include Plato, Descartes, Frege, and Wittgenstein. But many other examples are introduced by a current author and continued through comments, criticisms, and expansions in journals without credit being given to the originator. This is part of the methodology of the field; such uses are not considered plagiarism even though the examples might

have required much ingenuity to construct and were essential to the philosophical argument. In other fields, examples and other means of illustra-
tion are credited and are sometimes even named after the author; visual
illusions in psychology and the use of staining procedures in biology are
examples. Photographs and illustrations may be protected by copyright.
The kind of work that must be credited to the originator depends on the
field. The connection between what is considered an essential aspect of a
contribution is loosely tied to the conventions of crediting. Students who
are learning about the methodology of a field also must learn the difference between plagiarism and building on past ideas.

Advertisements appear on college campuses and in student newspapers
from mail-order term paper services. They offer term papers "typed and
ready for submission." One service claims a library of fifteen thousand papers and facilities for writing a custom paper to any specifications. Some
ads guarantee grades of B or better, failing which they promise to refund
the cost of the paper. Most students and faculty members will not hesitate
to condemn the use of term paper services. The services themselves often
acknowledge their lack of respectability by sending papers in "plain brown
envelopes" and guaranteeing not to send duplicate papers to the same campus. However, there are some interesting similarities between the use of
term paper services and other activities that are not considered unethical.
Let us look at some of these activities and compare them with term paper
services.

The *Encyclopedia Britannica* offered to purchasers a service that would research and write papers on almost any topic. Many scholars engage in contract research, accepting money to investigate and report on a topic of interest to the client. Many research institutes do all or mostly contract
research for a variety of clients: government agencies, corporations, or individuals. Many trade books, both nonfiction and fiction, are researched or
(re)written by people who are paid by the listed authors. The assistance
sometimes is publicly acknowledged and sometimes is not.

How do these activities differ from the use of term paper services? In
each case the writing or ideas of one person are used by another, but it is
not the same as plagiarism. By accepting money for research or writing,
researchers give up their rights to the material. They sell the products of
their labor in the same way bakers do when they sell bread. The distinction
between repetitive and creative production does not seem to be the crucial
factor. In fact, the practice has a long history in the arts: Great Renaissance
artists signed paintings in which a considerable part of the work was done
by their anonymous assistants.

There is something about the way in which the client claims credit for the
purchased work that is important, but what is it? When friends show us the
house that "they" just redecorated, do we think them immoral if they fail to
mention the interior decorator they hired or the magazine article whose
guidance they followed? Probably not. We give credit to our friends be-

cause they had the judgment to select good advice and took responsibility for the implementation. Likewise, a corporate executive who hires a consulting firm to do research for a report may *chose* to attribute the research to the consultants in order to dilute responsibility or to increase its credibility, but in business practice the executive is not thought immoral if his or her signature is the only one that appears on it. Although it is possible that friends and business superiors may assume that the executive did the job unaided, their error is not caused by deceit.

Unlike these examples, there is a clear expectation that all the intellectual work for a term paper is done by the student alone. This is so because the main purposes of the work are to evaluate the student and serve as a learning experience. In the other examples, the main purpose of the work is some end other than the work itself.

Comparing credit given for work on term papers, corporate reports, and house decorating raises interesting questions. Where direct benefits to the originators are important—grades, royalties, or promotions—perhaps credits should be specified carefully. On the other hand, jealousy about credit and authorship may interfere with cooperative efforts. Thus, if the result is important and if teamwork should be encouraged, maybe the proprietary nature of authorship should be played down. What other factors may be involved? What other examples can you think of where crediting the worker is or is not important?

FACULTY-STUDENT RELATIONS

Whenever there are large gaps in a hierarchy of power, the potential for ethical problems increases. One of the largest gaps in the academic hierarchy lies between students and faculty. In both undergraduate and graduate or professional schools, instructors have the power to grade; award financial support; provide guidance, research facilities, and recommendations for future placement; and approve or disapprove, thus determining success or failure. In the preceding section we explained how even the most objective means for judgments still allow biased evaluations, and most of the ways in which instructors evaluate students unavoidably involve subjective judgments. Subjective judgment allows the possibility of unfairness through carelessness, unconscious effects, or even deliberate bias.

Most of the time, at least for undergraduates, the interaction between student and instructor is restricted to the classroom and an occasional office consultation of short duration. In these cases the relationship of student to instructor is limited to professional contact, decreasing the likelihood that any judgment the instructor makes about the student will be based on academically irrelevant factors. But what happens when the relationship goes beyond the classroom?

Many undergraduate institutions encourage additional contact between instructors and students through social events, faculty participation in student residences, and so on. Graduate students, who have closer working relationships with the faculty, frequently interact with faculty members outside ordinary academic settings: department parties, the tennis court, or professional meetings, for example. Many instructors invite students to their homes. Such contact can enrich the learning experience, but it also endangers the impartiality of evaluations. The friendships or animosities that develop may affect the evaluative judgments that instructors make.

Although fictional accounts usually portray romantic relations between teachers and students in a positive light, such relationships offer great potential for unfair bias and exploitation. Faculty members are likely to be much older than their students, have more experience, and are in a position to take advantage of the student's respect and admiration. Students, flattered by attention from someone with prestige and authority, are particularly vulnerable. The difficulty of impartially grading a student-lover is obvious. Suppose the student deserves to fail or does badly on the final exam after a lovers' quarrel. Suppose the student is competing for a scholarship and the instructor is on the awarding committee.

Although colleges may disapprove of instructors becoming romantically involved with their students, they are usually careful to avoid interfering in the personal lives of the faculty. Although it is very likely that an instructor would be biased toward or against a student who is also a lover, and although the instructor's position of power over the student easily permits exploitation in a sexual relationship, there is a great reluctance to assume that bias and exploitation do exist. In many schools faculty-student romances are considered innocent until proven guilty (or scandalous). In fact, the danger of bias and exploitation exists whether the relationship is sexually intimate or not. Even people who disapprove of faculty-student romances do not usually see that the same dangers exist in faculty-student friendships. Students can use friendship to try to improve their grades, or they can be exploited by their teachers.

The structure of institutions of higher education involves great differences in power, and where there are great differences in power, there is great danger that relationships across different levels in the hierarchy can be exploitative. There is considerable precedent outside of academia for discouraging romantic liaisons when one person has power over or must judge another. Military organizations prohibit socializing across the ranks. Many institutions and corporations have nepotism laws prohibiting close relatives from occupying positions where one is the supervisor or evaluator of the other. Are these situations different from faculty-student relations? Are the differences morally relevant? Should limitations be placed on the relationships that faculty members may have with students? If so, what kind of restrictions should they be? Does the *potential* for abuse justify restrictions on personal freedom?

One professor was having a sexual relationship independently with two current students. Both relationships apparently began with mutual attraction. After a time, both students tried to end the relationships. The professor, angry and hurt by the rejections, threatened the students with noncooperation in their academic work. Eventually the students complained, news of the scandal began to spread, and disciplinary action was taken against the faculty member. Would the students' complaints have been as likely to provoke such action if the professor had made no overt threat? If there had been only one student involved and therefore less scandal? Compare this case with the more common and subtler form of sexual harassment in which students feel pressure to submit to relatively mild gestures such as an arm around the shoulder or suggestive banter. Some institutions of higher education have published official statements on sexual harassment, trying to call attention to the connection between the subtle and the blatant forms.

There is no question that both sexual harrassment and prostitution for grades are morally reprehensible, the first because a person is compelled to perform or submit to something that should be firmly in the realm of personal choice, the second because it deliberately corrupts the fairness of the evaluative process. But only rarely is a sexual relationship between a faculty member and a student a clear case of either practice. The problem is that the idealization of romance (our belief that people "fall for" rather than choose their romantic partners) helps veil the moral dangers of faculty-student romances.

In Chapter 4 we mentioned that the power instructors have over students may be abused when students are asked to serve as research subjects. Because the ethics of research with human subjects has received much attention, this potential for abuse is well known, and precautions have been taken to prevent its occurrence. However, students commonly assist faculty members in both research and teaching in many ways, serving as graders, laboratory assistants, or library researchers. Sometimes students are paid for their help, but often they work as volunteers, or scholar's apprentices. Ideally, the effort they contribute is rewarded by the knowledge and experience gained in assisting the faculty member.

But as with any apprentice system there is a danger of exploitation. Student assistants often do the most menial jobs in research and teaching: recording data, distributing questionnaires, scoring multiple choice exams, and even typing faculty correspondence. These are the kinds of things they learn the least from doing. Some colleges accept students from economically and educationally deprived backgrounds who need all the time they can get to catch up academically to their more privileged classmates. These students are given part-time jobs at low wages, running mimeograph machines and doing other menial tasks. Such practices, which seem to be exploitation, are defended with the argument that the menial tasks are essential to the operation of the institution, that faculty time is too valuable to spend on such tasks, or that the more important and intellectually challenging aspects of teaching and research demand the greater experience of the faculty person. Somebody has to do the job, and it is more fair, or has better consequences, to have students do it rather than anyone else. But this defense does not consider the needs of the students. For a few students the labor invested when serving as an apprentice can be returned severalfold when the student in turn becomes a faculty member, and so the indentured servitude may not be really onerous. However, most students do not become academics with the privilege of having apprentices. With menial tasks that need to be done and a captive population of students willing to do them, many schools succumb to the temptation and exploit their students.

SUMMARY

In this chapter we discussed some of the ethical problems that arise in teaching. The Principle of Fairness plays a central role in many of them. First we discussed college admissions and recruiting policies, which are areas that have been troubled by diminishing financial and population resources. We saw how selective admissions may conflict with equal opportunity. We discussed criteria for admissions beyond intellectual merit and the arguments that such criteria are fair. We saw how sex quotas are defended and supported and how special arguments defend the exclusion of men from women's colleges. Next we discussed the arguments for geographical and ethnic diversity and for favoring the children of alumni. The next section discussed how colleges decide on curricula and their responsibility and control versus the student's freedom to choose a program of study. It also looked at the instructor's freedom to choose topics and texts, the values inherent in every choice, and the possibility of biased or misleading course material. Then, in the context of the Principle of Fairness, we examined some of the problems that arise when students are evaluated, including the influence of bias on subjective judgment, how "objective" exams cannot be totally free from subjective evaluation, grade "curving," rewarding effort and improvement, and grade inflation. Next we analyzed cheating, with emphasis on two examples: plagiarism and term paper ghostwriting services. The last topic in the chapter is student-faculty relations. We talked about the effect of the power difference between students and faculty and its potential for abuse in friendships, romantic and sexual liaisons, and the exploitation of student labor.

Chapter 6

An Open End

We opened this book with a discussion of the Ivory Tower Myth—the belief that academia is a sheltered place whose occupants are dedicated to abstract issues, free from the cares and moral dilemmas of the ordinary world. The myth can be comforting and pleasing, but this does not make it true.

The material in this book is inconsistent with the myth. Higher education is filled with conflicting principles and moral dilemmas. But instead of replacing comfort with disillusionment and gloom, we want to leave you with more constructive options.

Dispelling the Ivory Tower Myth enables us to see more clearly. Rather than be discouraged because the myth is gone, we should, in the spirit of the pursuit of knowledge, be glad that the pretense has vanished. The comfort of the Ivory Tower Myth was undependable and illusory. The victims of injustice and unfairness are not able to ignore the problems; the myth only makes their situation worse. Making decisions while ignoring ethical issues can erode one's sensitivity and self-respect. Now we can directly confront issues that used to be ignored and work toward a better understanding and resolution of them.

In this small book we have presented a sample of the large range of moral problems that exist in higher education. Although many of these problems also arise in nonacademic settings, they are manifest in special ways in academia. We hope that this book will encourage people to think constructively about ethical problems in higher education: to recognize that they exist, to try to solve them, to work on the theoretical issues they raise, and to have greater sympathy and understanding for those who are affected by them.

In closing, we would like to suggest a few areas in which people involved with higher education can deal with the ethical issues raised in this book either by seeking practical solutions or by working on the conceptual issues involved in order to gain a better understanding of the source of the problems.

Many of the problems we have raised result from differences in power and influence in academia: the hierarchical structure of faculty ranks, the relation of teachers to students, and the effect of outside funding on research and educational directions. By recognizing that differences in power create ethical dangers, we can become more conscious of the misuse of power and work toward creating safeguards and structures that prevent some misuses.

Most schools have standing committees and grievance procedures for tenure and promotion decisions but not for dealing with other injustices that may occur. Some institutions have recently appointed ombudspeople to deal with problems that have no standard channels for redress. With new awareness of ethical issues, the roles of grievance committees or ombudspeople might be expanded to assist the powerless in difficult situations, to give guidance to the powerful, and to mediate in ethical conflicts.

Another general area of moral problems involves cheating and dishonesty. Public revelations of faculty research fraud and our own interviews suggest that this is a serious problem. A 1984 study of students at a major state university found that 78 percent admitted to cheating, and "similar studies show that cheating in college is on the rise nationally" (Hempel 1984). Pursuit of the credentials of research publication and grades can threaten the pursuit of knowledge for its own sake.

Academic dishonesty can be reduced either by making it harder to get away with or by reducing the pressures that encourage it. Policing and punishing are hard to do and are not in the spirit of the pursuit of knowledge. The pressures to cut corners, misrepresent, and take undeserved credit need to be given more attention and relieved rather than ignored or denied. It is difficult for institutions of higher education to admit that cheating or fraud has occurred because these practices are antithetical to the academic spirit and threaten the reputation of the institution. But unless more attention is given to these pressures in order to lessen them, the wrongs will continue and perhaps get worse. Just as other fields try to deal with abuses by creating internal structures for checking them, so also should academia create procedures to lessen the occurrence of dishonesty. We also need some study of the causes and effects of cheating and fraud. How widespread is research fraud and undeserved credit? How does it affect those who do it, those who know about it, and those who are hurt by it? How can evaluation procedures be changed to lessen the temptation to cheat? What does cheating do to morale in a classroom? To the attitude of a conscientious teacher? How does the organization of exams, discussions, and grading to eliminate cheating affect what is taught? We know that emphasis on evaluation creates pressures and temptations for immoral behavior. How necessary are the current evaluation procedures for the academic goals of higher education? What alternative procedures might there be? Could the bases for evaluation be changed so that moral value and responsiveness to public needs would not be overlooked?

Discussions about cheating and methodology raise interesting issues in epistemology and the philosophy of science. We need a closer look at how the methodology of a field defines legitimate and illegitimate research, how it determines what counts as plagiarism, and how what counts as plagiarism and research credit in turn affects the methodology. Perhaps these distinctions should be taught explicitly in courses instead of assuming that anyone with a basic moral sense can avoid cheating.

We have discussed how personal values are involved in the selection of exam questions and research questions and in the assumptions as well as the implications of our theories. Philosophers of science have written about how values affect theories and the development of science, but these philosophers concentrate on arguments about the existence of values, about what to do about them, or about the implications for scientific progress and ideals. We also need to ask how particular values, such as moral values, affect scientific research and how changes in moral awareness may change the direction of science.

Another area that needs more attention is the relationship between the institution and the public. Many academics argue that other professions and businesses should care more about their effect on the public and should be morally responsible for their products and for contributing to the quality of life of the community. Perhaps academics too should care more about their products—the results of their research and their teaching—and be held accountable for their effects.

We also need to look at problems that were not raised in this book. For example, the problem of copyright infringement was not mentioned although it is an important one for higher education, whose members are both major victims and major infringers. Copyrights raise fundamental problems about the nature of rights, ownership, and fairness.

We can also ask more fundamental questions. Do academic values require hierarchical structures? Do hierarchical structures necessarily imply power differences? Could alternative structures within the institution, even nonhierarchical structures, lessen these problems? Would they raise other ethical problems? How might outside funding sources be guided by academic values? What changes in their structure would be required? Why does academia adhere so tightly to confidentiality and secrecy in the evaluations of faculty members, students, and manuscripts submitted for publication? Are scholarly judges and referees more open and truthful or are they less responsible and accountable because of confidentiality? Is secrecy destructive to the pursuit of truth?

These suggestions are tentative. Much more could be said if we had clearer ideas about what the moral obligations of higher education are. There are several areas where the moral issues are complex, and although decisions may seem easy in extreme cases, we need to examine the complexities and give more study to the many factors involved.

We need to find out more about academic values themselves. We have assumed that academic goals are based on the advancement of knowledge. But like moral values, academic values may be created by a number of principles, some of which occasionally conflict or compete. Questions about academic values—whether knowledge is a means or an end and whether it is to be measured by its consequences or by its intrinsic worth—are similar to basic questions in ethics. Epistemology has been concerned with the existence and nature of knowledge but not with the basis for its value. We need to understand better how different kinds of knowledge are related to questions of value.

Giving attention to the ethical problems in higher education raises these and other questions, and the raising of questions—the challenge of problems that need attention—is the essence of academic life. Instead of bemoaning the existence of ethical problems or trying to ignore them, we can take them as a challenge to work on, to discover others, to open up new areas of study. What makes higher education rewarding and attractive is not that it has fewer ethical problems than the rest of the world but that its very nature embodies the hope of understanding them, of finding better explanations and sometimes even solutions.

References

ADAMS, R. *The Plague Dogs.* New York: Knopf, 1978.

ALLEN, G. *The Agile Administrator.* Tempe, Ariz.: Tempe Publishers, 1979.

AMERICAN PSYCHOLOGICAL ASSOCIATION. *Ethical Standards of Psychologists.* Washington, D.C.: Author, 1972.

AMERICAN PSYCHOLOGICAL ASSOCIATION. *Ethical Principles in the Conduct of Research with Human Participants: Report of the Ad-Hoc Committee of Ethical Standards in Psychology.* Washington, D.C.: Author, 1973.

BALTZELL, E. *The Protestant Establishment: Aristocracy and Class in America.* New York: Random House, 1964.

BARBER, T. *Pitfalls in Human Research.* New York: Pergamon, 1976.

BOK, D. *Beyond the Ivory Tower: Social Responsibilities of the Modern University.* Cambridge, Mass.: Harvard University Press, 1982.

BROAD, W. "Harvard Delays in Reporting Fraud." *Science,* Vol. 215 (Jan. 29, 1982), pp. 478–482.

BROAD, W. "Report Absolves Harvard in Case of Fakery." *Science,* Vol. 215 (Feb. 12, 1982), pp. 874–876.

BRUSH, S. "Should History of Science Be Rated X?" *Science,* Vol. 183, (March 22, 1974), pp. 1164–1172.

BUTTERFIELD, F. "Blacks Decrease but Women Increase on University Faculties." *New York Times,* January 28, 1984, p. 6.

CANUTESON, J. "We Can Help Eliminate Plagiarism by Teaching Students What It Is?" *Chronicle of Higher Education,* March 16, 1983, p. 30.

COHEN, J. *Chance, Luck, and Skill: The Psychology of Guessing and Gambling.* Baltimore, Md.: Penguin, 1960.

COHEN, J. *Behavior in Uncertainty.* London: Allen and Unwin, 1964.

COLE, S., AND J. COLE. "Scientific Output and Recognition: A Study of the Reward System in Science." *American Sociological Review,* Vol. 32 (1967), pp. 377–390.

CONWAY, J. "Yes: [Women's Colleges] Teach Self-Confidence." *New York Times Educational Supplement,* November 13, 1977, Educ. p. 13.

CORNELL, E. quoted in *Cornell University Announcements,* Vol. 74, No. 4 (July 15, 1982), Office of University Publications, Cornell University, Ithaca, N.Y.

CULLITON, B. "Coping with Fraud: The Darsee Case." *Science,* Vol. 220 (April 1, 1983), pp. 31–35.

DOLMATCH, T., ed. *Information Please Almanac.* New York: Simon & Schuster, 1981.

FABER, B. "The Sloan-Kettering Affair." Letter to the editor. *Science,* Vol. 185 (August 30, 1974), p. 734.

FIELDS, C. "Professors' Demands for Credit as 'Co-Authors' of Student Research Projects May Be Rising." *Chronicle of Higher Education*, Sept. 14, 1983, pp. 7, 10.

FRANKENA, W. AND J. GRANROSE. *Introductory Readings in Ethics*. Englewood Cliffs, N.J.: Prentice Hall, 1974.

FRANKENA, W. *Ethics*. Englewood Cliffs, N.J.: Prentice Hall, 1979.

GOLDSMITH, D., ed. *Scientists Confront Velikovsky*, Ithaca, N.Y.: Cornell University Press, 1977.

HARDING, S., AND M. HINTIKKA. eds. *Discovering Reality*. Synthese Library. Dordrecht: Reidel Press, 1983.

HEMPEL, M. quoted in "In Brief," *Chronicle of Higher Education*, Vol. XXVII, No. 23 (February 15, 1984), p. 2.

HUNT, M. "Research through Deception." *New York Times Magazine*, September 12, 1982, pp. 66–67+.

KAHANE, H. *Logic and Contemporary Rhetoric*. Belmont: Wadsworth, Calif.: 1984.

KELMAN, H., AND C. HOVLAND. "Reinstatement of the Communicator in Delayed Measurement of Opinion Change." *Journal of Abnormal and Social Psychology*, Vol. 48 (1953), pp. 327–335.

KOESTLER, A. *The Case of the Midwife Toad*. New York: Random House, 1971.

KUHN, T. *The Structure of Scientific Revolutions*. Chicago: University of Chicago Press, 1962.

LEHRER, T. *Too Many Songs by Tom Lehrer*. New York: Pantheon, 1981, pp. 125, 154.

LEVEY, R. "MIT Role in Research for Military Questioned." *Boston Globe*, August 7, 1983, p. 16.

LUDLUM, R. *The Matlock Paper*. New York: Dell, 1974.

MASSACHUSETTS STATE LEGISLATURE. Chapter 271, Section 50, Laws of Massachusetts. *Annotated Laws of Massachusetts*. Rochester, N.Y.: The Lawyers Co-operative Publishing Co., 1980, p. 619. (Reprint.)

MASSON, J. *The Assault on Truth: Freud's Suppression of the Seduction Theory*. New York: Farrar, Strauss & Giroux, 1984.

McCAIN, G., AND E. SEGAL. *The Game of Science*. Belmont, Calif.: Brooks/Cole, 1969.

MEHLER, J., AND T. BEVER. Editorial: *Cognition: International Journal of Cognitive Psychology*, Vol. 2/1 (1973), pp. 7–11.

MERTON, R. "Priorities in Scientific Discovery: A Chapter in the Sociology of Science." *American Sociological Review*, Vol. 22 (1957), pp. 635–659.

MILGRAM, S. "Behavioral Study of Obedience." *Journal of Abnormal and Social Psychology*, Vol. 67 (1963), pp. 371–378.

MOULTON, J. *The Guidebook for Publishing Philosophy*, Newark, Del.: American Philosophical Association, 1975.

ROBINSON, G. "Simulations of Scientific Discovery: Pattern Fitting versus Pattern Finding," (Paper presented to the Department of Psychology, University of Kentucky, Lexington, 1979).

SCARR-SALAPATEK, S. "Race, Social Class and IQ." *Science*, Vol. 174 (December 24, 1971), pp. 1285–1295.

SHAW, P. "Plagiary." *American Scholar*, Summer 1982, pp. 325–337.

SINGER, P. *Animal Liberation: A New Ethics for Our Treatment of Animals*. New York: Random House, 1975.

SINGER, P. *Practical Ethics*. Cambridge: Cambridge University Press, 1979.

SKINNER, B. *Beyond Freedom and Dignity*. New York: Knopf, 1972.

SWAZEY, J., AND S. SCHER. "The Whistleblower as Deviant Professional: Professional Norms and Responses to Fraud in Clinical Research," (Presented at the Workshop on Whistleblowing in Biomedical Research, Washington, D.C., 1981).

THOMAS, M. Personal communication, 1983.

TITTLE, C., AND A. ROWE. "Moral Appeal, Sanction Threat, and Deviance: An Experimental Test." *Social Problems*, Vol. 20 (1973), pp. 488–498.

TULLOCK, G. *The Organization of Inquiry.* Durham, N.C.: Duke University Press, 1966.

United States Supreme Court Reports, Vol. 57, L. Ed. 2d, (1979), pp. 750–853.

VAN DEN BERGHE, P. *Academic Gamesmanship.* New York: Abelard-Schuman, 1970.

VELIKOVSKY, I. *Worlds in Collision.* Garden City, N.Y.: Doubleday, 1950.

VESEY, G. "The Princess and the Philosopher," *Reason and Responsibility*, ed. J. Feinberg. Belmont, Calif.: Wadsworth, 1981, pp. 245–250.

VETTER, B., AND E. BABCO. *Professional Women and Minorities: A Manpower Data Resource Guide*, Washington, D.C.: Scientific Manpower Commission, 1981.

WALLACH, L., AND M. WALLACH. *Psychology's Sanction of Selfishness: The Error of Egoism in Theory and Therapy.* San Francisco: W. H. Freeman, 1983.

WESTFALL, R. "Newton and the Fudge Factory." *Science.* Vol. 179 (1973), pp. 751–758.

WINKLER, K. "Faculty Wary of Plan to Close Utah College, Change Its Name, and Reopen a Day Later." *Chronicle of Higher Education*, February 23, 1983, p. 11.

WOLFF, R. "Chapter 5: Normative Ethical Theories." *Introductory Philosophy.* Englewood Cliffs, N.J.: Prentice Hall, 1979.

ZAJONC, R. "Attitudinal Effects of Mere Exposure." *Journal of Personality and Social Psychology Monograph Supplement*, Vol. 9 (1968), pp. 1–27.

Name Index

A

Adams, R., 57
Allen, G., 39
Aristotle, 5

B

Babco, E., 40
Bakke, A., 76
Baltzell, E., 74
Barber, T., 67
Bever, T., 61
Bok, D., 1
Braunwald, E., 70
Broad, W., 67
Brush, S., 66
Burt, C., 64
Butterfield, F., 40

C

Canuteson, J., 89
Cohen, J., 54
Cole, J., 60
Cole, S., 60
Conway, J., 75
Cornell, E., 78–79
Culliton, B., 70

D

Darsee, J., 66–67, 70
Descartes, R., 82
Dolmatch, T., 75

E

Elizabeth of Bohemia, 82
Elizabeth II, 82

F

Faber, B., 67–68
Fields, C., 70
Frankena, W., 5
Frege, G., 89
Freud, S., 60, 64

G

Galileo, 58
Goldsmith, D., 63
Granrose, J., 5

H

Harding, S., 9
Hempel, M., 96
Hintikka, M., 9
Hitler, A., 68
Hovland, C., 89
Hughes, H., 68
Hume, D., 5
Hunt, M., 56

J

Jagger, M., 82

Subject Index